What Your Colleagues Are Saying . . .

"I have been involved in the implementation of Social and Emotional Learning (SEL) in schools for many years. What I loved about this book is that it takes the theory and research behind SEL and puts heart and relevance behind it. It not only gives practical advice and suggestions, but also serves as a kind and gentle way for the readers to reflect on their own practice and work to grow their own social and emotional skills. I have already recommended it to classroom teachers and am envisioning how I will use it for the next professional development activity I will be facilitating, as this book can be relevant to classroom teachers, administrators, and anyone in a school setting who works with kids. The title is *Start With the Heart* and I feel like the heart of the author, her love for students, and her passion for this work comes through on every page."

Victoria Blakeney, Director of Student Support
Renton School District, WA

"Educators have known that building students' social emotional skills (SES) is critical to their future success. It's time for schools to embrace and understand the significance of being deliberate in incorporating SES skills in their classrooms and schools. Hats off to Michelle L. Trujillo for writing a book that walks teachers and schools through a process that shows how it can be successfully done."

Kim Campbell, Middle School Teacher and Dean of Students
Hopkins West Junior High, Minnetonka, MN

"*Start With the Heart* is a must-read for teachers seeking research-based practices that expand the social, emotional, and academic development of their students."

Steve Canavero, PhD, Superintendent of Public Instruction
Nevada Department of Education

"Michelle L. Trujillo skillfully blends research, evidence, anecdotes, and opportunities for readers' personal reflections. She has produced an excellent resource that appeals to the intellectual mind, common sense, and the reader's heart. This fantastic book separates itself from others by not only backing up claims with evidence and research, but also facilitating the reader in arriving at those very same conclusions through logic, common sense, and personal reflection into his or her own life experience with social and emotional learning. It has been said that you must touch the heart before you can teach the mind. This book does both."

Gregg Iha, District Resource Teacher
Hawaii Department of Education

"This is a powerful and moving resource and will inspire every educator who wants to make a difference!"

Eric Jensen, Author and Educational Consultant
Jensen Learning

"Chock-full of validating and affirming statements for best practice when supporting students who have experienced trauma, this book presents great probing questions to use with staff. Michelle L. Trujillo provides powerful questions that support leaders in framing meaningful and reflective conversations. After reading Chapter 2, I used some of those questions the next week. I needed this read after a busy start to the school year. Our students need us to be our best selves!

As a fellow continuation high school principal, I read this book and felt heard and seen. The work, the reminders, and belief systems outlined by Michelle inspire me to keep learning, improving, and implementing social and emotional learning for students and staff."

Amy Lloyd, Principal
Adelante Continuation High School, CA

"Through touching anecdotes and practical activities, Trujillo's strengths-based approach conveys feasible strategies for improving schools: start with positive regard, teach the social-emotional skills we want to see, and model these skills for students and colleagues."

Kent McIntosh, Professor,
University of Oregon

"We are finally beginning to recognize that schools cannot focus on academics alone. The success of children is tied to their social and emotional development. This important book describes what schools can do to address the needs of the whole child. For educators and others who seek to ensure that schools are able to respond to the needs of our children, this book is an invaluable resource."

Pedro A. Noguera, PhD, Distinguished Professor of Education
UCLA Graduate School of Education & Information Studies

"This is a very important book. It is well written, insightful, practical, and consistent with research on the science of learning and development. *Start With the Heart* strategically incorporates the voices of students and provides readers with opportunities to reflect so that they can embed social emotional learning in their practices and 'way of being.' Learning and teaching is hard—particularly when students face many challenges. However, students and teachers can succeed; this book illustrates how we can create safe, engaging, equitable learning opportunities for all students."

David Osher, Vice President and Institute Fellow
American Institutes for Research

"Michelle L. Trujillo brings a scientifically-based framework to this work, as well as a strong social and emotional component, both of which are so important to our schools. Michelle is able to bridge the gap so all stakeholders understand the impact that creating a social and emotional learning environment has on academic achievement."

Dr. Greta Peay, Chief Officer, Instructional Services
Clark County School District, NV

"Michelle L. Trujillo takes you on a journey with Social and Emotional Learning to make a difference: not like on a train ride that keeps you on track, but more like an airplane flight that takes you to places you may never have been before. Her Reflection Pages, Suggestions From Students, and Study Questions, peppered with a strong dose of Hope, guide you toward your destination to becoming a better educator. Enjoy the ride!"

Dr. Stephen Sroka, President of Health Education
Consultants and Founder of "The Power of One"

"Michelle L. Trujillo writes compellingly about leading with heart and intentionality toward a systematic approach to social and emotional learning (SEL). She elevates the critical voices of students and shares concrete strategies to help educators create schools that simultaneously meet the social, emotional, and economic needs of young people and adults."

Karen Van Ausdal, Senior Director of Practice
The Collaborative for Academic, Social, and Emotional Learning (CASEL)

Start With the Heart

This book is written for my husband, David

and

it is inspired by ALL who are ASPIRE.

Start With the Heart

Igniting Hope in Schools Through Social and Emotional Learning

Michelle L. Trujillo

CORWIN

FOR INFORMATION:

Corwin

A SAGE Company

2455 Teller Road

Thousand Oaks, California 91320

(800) 233-9936

www.corwin.com

SAGE Publications Ltd.

1 Oliver's Yard

55 City Road

London EC1Y 1SP

United Kingdom

SAGE Publications India Pvt. Ltd.

B 1/I 1 Mohan Cooperative Industrial Area

Mathura Road, New Delhi 110 044

India

SAGE Publications Asia-Pacific Pte Ltd

18 Cross Street #10-10/11/12

China Square Central

Singapore 048423

Program Director: Jessica Allan

Content Development Editor: Lucas Schleicher

Senior Editorial Assistant: Mia Rodriguez

Production Editor: Tori Mirsadjadi

Copy Editor: Amy Marks

Typesetter: C&M Digitals (P) Ltd.

Proofreader: Sue Irwin

Indexer: Beth Nauman-Montana

Cover Designer: Candice Harman

Marketing Manager: Margaret O'Connor

Library of Congress Cataloging-in-Publication Data

Names: Trujillo, Michelle L., 1967- author.

Title: Start with the heart : igniting hope in schools through social and emotional learning / Michelle L. Trujillo.

Description: Thousand Oaks, California : Corwin, 2019. | Includes bibliographical references and index.

Identifiers: LCCN 2018048435 | ISBN 9781544352824 (pbk. : alk. paper)

Subjects: LCSH: Affective education. | Social learning. | Self-consciousness (Awareness) | Teachers—Conduct of life. | Teacher-student relationships.

Classification: LCC LB1072 .T78 2019 | DDC 370.15/34—dc23

LC record available at https://lccn.loc.gov/2018048435

This book is printed on acid-free paper.

SUSTAINABLE FORESTRY INITIATIVE **Certified Chain of Custody**
At Least 10% Certified Forest Content
www.sfiprogram.org
SFI-01028

22 23 24 25 10 9 8 7 6 5 4

Contents

Visit the companion website at
resources.corwin.com/StartWithTheHeart
for downloadable resources.

Preface

Ignite Hope Now!

Education is our calling
In our students, we believe
We're giving everything we've got
Yet still, some don't achieve

We see kids living in adversity
In the light of each tomorrow
Experiences we can't imagine
Such hurt and fear and sorrow

Academics are important,
Yes, test scores must be improved
But kids will find it tough to learn
If they are hungry, hurting, or abused

So much falls upon our shoulders
More placed on our plates each day
Yet in our hands, our students rest
We can help them find their way

As we embark upon our lessons
Of reading, writing, science, and math
We can ignite hope for our young people
If we place character upon their path

You see,
We can teach them through our actions,
To be human above all things
To serve others with love and integrity
And feel the joy and hope this brings

And hope is certainly essential
In the lives of all our kids
But it is up to us to ignite it
To light the flame that lives within

It starts with understanding
That their lives are not like ours
We must meet them where they are today
Find their strengths, then raise the bar

It is not up to us to "fix them"
Or correct what's tough at home
But we can teach them to accept themselves
And help them know they're not alone

We can love them and respect them,
Teach them to act responsibly,
We can model compassion and acceptance
And challenge them to think more critically

It's not up to us to change them,
Rather, the environment in which they learn
Let our classrooms be their safe place,
To question, explore, discern

We can truly make a difference
Starting with the Heart, our fervent vow
And with SEL as the foundation
We can ignite HOPE in our schools now!

About the Author

Michelle L. Trujillo, MEd, is an author, inspirational speaker, and educational consultant. "Mrs. T," as she is known to her students and reading audience, makes a tangible, sustainable, and positive difference through her books, keynotes, and training seminars. She shares enthusiasm, experience, and applicable takeaways with her audience, while she imparts a philosophy that ignites hope in schools and the workplace. Named Nevada's 2017 Innovative Educator of the Year, Michelle has appeared on television (including *Oprah*) and radio across the nation as a guest expert. Her keynotes and trainings leave audiences enthused, inspired, deeply touched, and wanting more. Feel free to contact Michelle at www.ignitinghopenow.com to schedule her as a speaker or workshop leader.

Introduction

Social, Emotional, and Academic Development: A Way of Being

S he was obviously tired. She came to school that morning appearing dirty and disheveled. But, she came to school. Through tears of frustration, she explained she had slept on a park bench the night before. She had tried to go home, but her mom was doing a drug deal and locked her out of the house. So, she walked to the park and eventually fell asleep on a bench, alone and cold. When the sun came up, she walked to school. Her mom didn't know where she was, and in her opinion, her mom didn't care ... but, she came to school. Why? Why did she choose to show up, when others might have chosen to go to a friend's house or wander aimlessly? Because it wasn't just about school, it was that *at* school, she was connected. This beautifully rebellious, wildly stubborn, and woefully broken-hearted teenager came to school because she knew that we expected her, that we wanted her, and that we cared. This connection she felt did not happen naturally. It was a connection born in intention and effort. Connection that makes a difference in the lives of human beings must be conscientious. To be conscientious is to be mindful, intentional, or attentive. To truly be connected, we need to start with the heart in a true effort to see others for who they are on the inside, and appreciate and value them as such. This is imperative in the school setting, because when we as educators sincerely connect with each other and with our students, we set a tone for belonging, living, and learning that is impactful and potentially life-changing.

As I look back on my career as a teacher and an administrator, I realize I was blessed to live and love my vocation. To me, it was never a job, or work I dreaded. Instead, it inspired me, filled me with joy. I believe there was a reason for this. The students at the alternative education high school where I served as a principal said it best. When asked why they were able to find success at our school when most had not achieved academically nor personally prior to enrolling with us, one word resounded again and again: *family*! They said that when they became students at our school, they felt accepted into a family that would love them, hold them to high expectations, and provide them with a second chance. That doesn't mean it was easy or that immediate positive change occurred. Yet, our school family provided the students, and staff for that matter, with a connection to something greater than themselves. We were connected by a common purpose as we aspired to pursue integrity, responsibility, and education. I use the word *we* purposely. The administration, counselors, teachers, paraprofessionals, custodians, support staff, students, parents, the school board, and community members all knew that *we* were stronger together than any of us were individually. We had more talents, expertise, and gifts when combined. We knew our chance for success increased exponentially when we chose to encourage, support, and challenge one another. We knew the road ahead would be rugged at times, and steep, because most of our students came to us from a place of adversity or trauma, yet we were steadfastly aware we would be okay, because we would travel the road together, sharing the challenges and the joy, the trials and the triumphs.

As you read this, you may be thinking, "What kind of school is this?" I can tell you . . . it is any school in which, regardless of its size, the human beings who inhabit it choose to make a conscientious connection by starting with the heart. It is any school in which the human beings who are the adults in the school environment choose to see the stories behind the human beings who are the students. In fact, it is any school in which the human beings who are the adults choose to see the story behind one another, and model for their students to do the same, so that people are met where they are, with every person seeking to understand before jumping to judgment. It is a school in which social and emotional learning is a philosophy in which all are invested, so that academic achievement has an opportunity to occur because the all-encompassing *we* are engaged and empowered to trust, to grow, and to learn.

If you are interested in this kind of school, please join me on a journey to explore the power of connection and the fundamentals of social and emotional learning and its impact on academic development. I have an idea of what you may be thinking. In fact, I'd guess that it sounds something like this: "I appreciate your invitation, but as much as I would like to go on this journey with you, I just have too much on my plate. I cannot add one more thing!" I've been there. I know the feeling. The expectations for educators and the pressures they face, regardless of their role, seem to get more demanding each day. New state and federal mandates, protocols for measurable outcomes for students and educators alike, and requirements for state assessments that correlate results with teacher or school performance create a sense of anxiety and heaviness that can permeate our halls, our classrooms, and our hearts. In addition, we are seeing more and more children with mental health issues, as well as those (children and adults) who are living with past or present trauma, and these things, too, fill our plate with the need for an emotional energy that can be beyond our capacity. But this is the very reason that you cannot afford to neglect this journey. In fact, the reminders, reflections, and discoveries that you will find within these pages will give you back time, and help you to be more effective and productive.

In Chapters 1 and 2, we will explore how the power of love and connection can impact an education system in a life-changing way. According to the Aspen Institute (2018),

> Schools must be safe, welcoming, and supportive spaces for student to learn and for them to feel a sense of belonging and the freedom to develop their own identity and sense of self. . . . Indeed, the greatness of public education lies in its promise to take all individuals and provide them with the opportunity to build the life they want. (pp. 1, 3)

As educators, we have the responsibility for creating an environment that will lead to a fulfilment of this promise for our students. I hope that these chapters will encourage you to value this responsibility. In Chapters 3–7, I present social and emotional learning as a process in which all of the human beings within the school system interact with compassion, sincere curiosity, high expectations, and respect in a way that builds relationships, fosters academic achievement, and provides for success in school and life. You will discover that social and emotional learning is not something to be added to your plate. It is your plate! In these chapters, I introduce various components of social, emotional, and academic development with applicable anecdotes and practical suggestions. Finally, Chapter 8 will both challenge you and validate the responsibility that lies in your hands as a person who has chosen to interact with young people on a daily basis. By the time you close this book, I hope you will be inspired with purpose and positivity, both personally and professionally, and will want to put into practice what you've learned.

Please consider this book as a conversation between us. I challenge you to invest in the conversation by leaving the periphery as the reader and interacting as a participant. Throughout the journey, you'll recognize the valuable qualities that already reside in your mind and heart; the messages found within the pages of this book are not unfamiliar to you. Rather, each word of encouragement, challenge, and guidance is meant to awaken and inspire your soul. There will be opportunities for you to write in this book: to reflect on your life, your experiences, and your instructional practices; to brainstorm with others; and to put specific ideas into practice. As I share anecdotes, experiences, philosophies, and strategies, I do not claim to have all of the answers. What I do claim is to be a person with a heart full of love and a desire to inspire all people within the school community to create connections with each other while exploring and embedding social, emotional, and academic learning principles into daily actions and behaviors. When we do this, we have an opportunity to make today a better day for ourselves and for our students. When we do this, we invest in each other so that the learning and living that takes place in our schools is inspired, engaging, and contagious. And, finally, when we do this, when we *start with the heart*, we honor humanity and value relationships, so that no human being feels as if he or she must sleep on a park bench, alone in the cold.

It's About the People

A "Meeting Them Where They Are" Mentality

When it comes to what matters in life, we all know it is about the people, not the things. Unfortunately, sometimes it takes a life-changing event, such as a serious illness or the death of a loved one, for us to appreciate that fact. We often get so caught up in the responsibilities of our everyday lives that we begin to focus on the "things" in our lives without even realizing it. We become preoccupied with checking off the tasks on our to-do lists, playing catch-up with household chores, or completing school-related work that spills over into the afternoons or weekends, and we neglect what is right there in front of us: people. More often than not, it is the people we are closest to whom we neglect the most. I speak from experience. There were times in my professional life as an administrator when I was so focused on completing evaluations or gathering data for accreditation that I unintentionally, and sometimes even subconsciously, neglected my husband and children. There were times when I was physically present but emotionally removed. As much as I would be disappointed in myself when I realized what I was doing, I also understood that I am human and sometimes needed a reminder to keep my priorities in order. Fortunately, my husband, who often knows me better than I know myself, was there to remind me.

IT'S ABOUT THE PEOPLE

Consider this chapter the reminder you may need. It is always and should always be about the people. Let's not wait for those extreme moments of illness, loss, or grief to trigger a wake-up call. As we set out on a journey to start with the heart, let's begin with our personal lives and consider those who are important to us. As I suggested in the introduction, throughout this book I will provide opportunities for reflection. Take time right now to reflect on and acknowledge the people in your personal life who are important and why they matter to you:

The People in Your Personal Life

Name: Reason:

_____

_____

_____

_____

_____

_____

_____

_____

_____

_____

I asked you to reflect on people in your personal life who matter to you because you must always keep them at the forefront of your mind and in your heart. Early in my teaching career, someone taught me the "five years from now" rule. For example, when in a dilemma between taking a sick day to stay home with my children or coming to work to teach a specific lesson, I would ask myself, "Five years from now, who will remember?" The answer, inevitably, was my children. My students wouldn't remember on which day I taught which lesson, but my son and daughter would definitely remember if I stayed home to cuddle them when they were little and not feeling well. We are better as educators and professionals when we keep what's first, first.

At the same time, we do spend a great deal of our time at school. There are people in our professional lives, too, who are important to us. This is interesting, because much like our families, we don't necessarily get to choose the people with whom we work. As a result, we tend to be drawn to those with whom we have things in common, be

it interests, philosophies, or personality traits. Can you create the same
for those in your professional life that you created for those in your pers

The People in Your Professional Life

Name: *Reason:*

_____

_____

_____

_____

_____

_____

_____

Furthermore, consider this: Whose list might *you* be on? If your students or colleagues were asked to create the same kind of list, would they include you? Please stop reading for a moment and contemplate these questions. Jot down anything significant that occurs to you:

_____

_____

_____

_____

_____

These exercises are important to reflect upon, because how we interact with those in our professional life and how they react to and interact with us is critical to this journey. Perhaps what is more telling in these reflection exercises is recognition of who is *not* on your list. There may be people within our work environments whom we do not identify as important to us, yet we are called to work professionally together and to treat each other with respect and dignity. Being compassionate and growth-minded toward all people within our workplace is necessary. Because we don't always get to choose our colleagues or our students, it is imperative that we accept the significance of understanding that *all of us*, our colleagues as well as the students, family members, and other associates of our school community, come from different experiences, cultures, opportunities, and abilities.

OUR DIVERSITY MAKES US STRONGER

It is crucial to understand that in many ways we are different, and that being different doesn't make us more than or less than. It just makes us different. Our differences, if honored, provide valuable insight that helps people to be more aware, well-rounded, and enlightened. Although we as human beings are uniquely different, we are alike in essential ways. Because of these similarities, our diversity makes us stronger.

Imagine the insight and enlightenment that could be found if all of humanity chose to appreciate our diversity. Instead, as a society, we tend to experience division. As much as we do not have control over all human beings, we can control our own perspectives, words, and actions. It is essential that we, as educators, understand that it is our choice to approach our professional life in this light, accepting each other and seeking to understand people from a place of love, regardless of skin color, religious affiliation, sexual orientation, gender preference, socioeconomic status, or ability. Moreover, until we do this, we will fall short in making meaningful connections. So, how do we initiate this outlook within our work environment?

MEETING PEOPLE WHERE THEY ARE

We have to start by meeting people where they are. Bryan Rhoades provided my first lesson in this regard. In middle school he was diagnosed with Friedreich ataxia, a type of muscular dystrophy that causes progressive damage to the nervous system. It manifested itself in Bryan's body by causing constant jerking movements of his arms and legs. I was in my first year as an adapted physical education teacher when I met Bryan. I was inspired by this student who was bound and determined to do things as he did them *before* this debilitating disease began to take control of his body. I have many memories of Bryan, who imprinted himself upon my heart from the moment I met him. With unbridled enthusiasm, he told me he was an amazing football player and someday he was going to play for his beloved Denver Broncos.

Though I was his teacher for only three years, he and I remained in each other's lives. His mom and aunt were on their own, raising Bryan and his little brother. They worked hard for these boys, trying to make ends meet, but they needed extra support sometimes, and my husband and I found ourselves helping out occasionally.

Toward the end of Bryan's life, just a year after he graduated from high school, I cherished time with him as he recalled fun memories from the hospital bed set up in his living room. He laughed out loud when he reminded me of the time I let him ride a bicycle through the middle of town. His balance was so poor that he had to go as fast as he could to keep the bike upright, all the while knowing he did not have the physical ability to stop the bike on his own. He teased me about how I could barely keep up with him as I ran alongside him to prevent him from crashing. I must have been crazy! Oh, but it was worth it to hear his laugh and see the joy in his face that came from the feeling of freedom as the wind touched his face. The independence of riding on his own gave Bryan a reprieve from his present reality, and I was so grateful to be there with him.

In my naiveté as a young teacher, I only knew to meet Bryan right where he was: stubborn, convicted, and fighting his disease with all his might! He taught me to see beyond his disability, beyond the seventh-grade student who didn't care much about his school work. He helped me to see his heart; he invited me, in attitude and spirit, to meet him there and to provide opportunities for him to accomplish small tasks and achieve what seemed to be impossible. Somehow, some way, I understood that although academic achievement was important to his life as a student, it would have to take a back seat to Bryan's need for independence, his desire to be the active kid he had always been, for just a bit longer.

Even today, my memories of Bryan influence my motivation to encourage educators to meet *all* colleagues and students where they are; to see *all* of them for the people they are as human beings, knowing that we may not comprehend the reason behind someone's way of being. We must attempt to see past a disconcerting behavior in order to seek an understanding of what happened in that person's life to cause such a response. This doesn't mean that we neglect to correct the behavior or disregard expectations for positive conduct, but such consequences or high expectations will be meaningless if we remain unaware of the catalyst that prompted the undesirable conduct.

Our students provide us with plenty of opportunities to put this quest for understanding into practice. Our youngest learners, especially, can test our patience because they frequently resort to "acting out" behavior when they don't have the words to articulate why they are upset or frustrated. Students in middle or high school may be capable of explaining their outbursts or negative actions, but they don't always *want* to share or verbalize. They may have protective factors in place, due to trauma, fear, or embarrassment, that prevent us, as educators, from being enlightened to the the story behind their behavior. As a result, it can be challenging for us to connect with these students.

In fact, the students we tend to have the greatest difficulty building relationships with, the ones who tend to be our repeat offenders with regard to discipline issues, disrespect, bullying, and the like—as well as the students who are often targets of such behavior—are frequently kids who live with the reality of adversity. Some act angry, tough, and self-righteous; others appear apathetic or rude. Author and educational leader Eric Jensen (2009) writes, "Behavior that comes off as apathetic or rude may actually indicate feelings of hopelessness and despair" (p. 29). Think about it. We see this behavior in our students. *Here's a challenge for you:* Try to see behind the façade, to determine what they might be feeling and thinking and find out why, even when they push you away. If we are persistent and accepting, we will connect with the hearts of our students. In doing so, we will set the foundation for trust that allows our students to feel seen and heard, which ultimately helps them know that they are people whom we care about and in whom we find worth.

Take Time to Learn

You may be wondering: How? How do I connect with a kid who is pushing me away? How do I connect, when in that very moment I'd rather scream? Or even, How am I supposed to connect with this kid, when right now, I don't even like him? These questions are based in the reality of day-to-day interactions with students who display behaviors that sometimes make us want to pull out our hair. I offer two solutions. First, we must take time to learn about our students. I recently spoke with an elementary school principal who said that he was going to encourage all of his teachers to write down three things that they knew about their students' lives outside of school. He emphasized that he did not want them to write what they assumed, but rather what they really knew. Inevitably there will be some students about whom teachers have no knowledge, other than their experience of those students at school. Gaining this knowledge will provide teachers with insight into the human being behind the behavior, the story behind the student. Seeking to learn more about our students is valuable in helping us, as educators, to better support, guide, and teach them so that they can make responsible choices.

Change the Questions

The second solution comes from a philosophy embedded in the teachings and practices of an organization called Creating the Future (2018). Hildy Gottlieb, cofounder of this organization, lives by the credo that, if we change the questions, we can change the world.

Have you ever really thought about the questions you ask? When our tough students act out or demonstrate behavior that we know may escalate, we tend to ask demanding questions such as, "Why did you do that?" or "What were you thinking?" These questions can put kids, and colleagues or employees for that matter, on the defensive. They naturally assume the question comes with a predetermined judgement or assessment of the situation and that, regardless of their answer, it will likely result in a negative consequence. Instead of getting answers, by asking these questions, we aggravate the situation inadvertently. To avoid doing so, we can replace the questions that we ask the student, colleague, or employee with a simple request: "Can you tell me more. . . ?" We can follow that up with ". . . about the situation," ". . . about how you're feeling right now," ". . . about what upset you?" or any other open-ended question appropriate to the situation. The *tell me more* request lets the person with whom we are talking know that we are willing to listen and that we want to understand what happened from his or her perspective. This is an ideal way to meet people exactly where they are in the moment, without jumping to conclusions or heightening any anxiety they may already have. When children or adults feel heard or encouraged, which this type of question allows, they are more open to connection and less likely to repeat the same negative behavior in the future. This does wonders for classroom management, but it can also have a lasting effect on a student's life as an adult.

You Were the First People to Tell Me I Could Be Somebody

Case in point, last year I received a letter from a former student who had struggled throughout middle and high school. In fact, she even dropped out for several months prior to enrolling in our school. She wrote to our staff after receiving her acceptance letter to a four-year university. Her letter is a testimony to the power of connection, support, and encouragement in the school system (see Figure 1.1).

FIGURE 1.1

Hello Everyone!

You were the first people that I wanted to tell that I was accepted into a four-year college! I will graduate this December from community college and walk with my Associate of Arts in the May ceremony. I'm going to be transferring to the university with a GPA of 3.3! Can you believe it? I have to say, when I got my letter of acceptance, I cried like a baby. I never imagined, me, an eighth-grade drop-out junkie, would be accepted into college. But I was! I remember you all telling me all of the things that I was capable of, like passing my classes and kicking drugs, and me thinking, "These people are crazy! I can't do any of those things!" You were right though. I can and I am doing it!

I want to thank you all for everything you did for me. I want you to know that I believe with everything in my soul that if I had never been blessed with the opportunity of having you all come into my life, and believing in me so

(Continued)

(Continued)

relentlessly, I would not be where I am today. You were my principal, my teachers, the school secretary and nurse, the custodians and the counselors and all of you took a stand for me and believed in me when nobody else in my life did, including myself. You were the first people to tell me that I could be somebody. You planted a seed in me years ago and with every year it grew, little by little, and when I was finally ready, that seed bloomed. When I struggled, you gave me the encouragement to know that I was better than the way that I was living. Because of that encouragement, I developed a sense of confidence that I never had before. It was this confidence, inspired by all of you, that enabled me to make an effort in school. Your love and high expectations helped me to realize that I was smart and could actually achieve in my classes. You made such a difference in my life and I feel so grateful to you for that. Being able to share my acceptance with you all makes me so proud!

I love you!
Kat

What Kat didn't say in her letter is that we taught her using our most engaging instructional strategies. We created academic and behavioral interventions—this was before they had official names as multi-tiered systems of support. We pushed her to achieve academically and helped her develop her decision-making skills. But, more important, what we did that made a sustainable difference in Kat's life was to take the time to see past her addiction and behind her truancy and her intermittent apathy, in order to believe in her potential. Sometimes, as educators, we forget the importance of this mentality as a crucial element of preparing our students to be college and career ready.

When I was a principal, I was blessed to work with a multitude of talented teachers. One such teacher, Ashlee Nicoll, was a master of the "meeting students where they are" mentality in order to help them see their potential. Mrs. Nicoll's reflection below is evidence of the positive difference this mentality can make in the life of a child:

Defeated, angry, deflated. These are the words that described Charlie the first time I met him. It was the summer of 2016 and Charlie was ready to drop out of high school and throw his life away. "I'll get some job and just work every day until I die." His outlook on what his life would be was dismal. He didn't believe success and accomplishment were things he could achieve in life; he didn't believe he deserved to have good things happen to him because his life up until this point had been a journey of pain, loss, and disappointment. Charlie had always struggled in school and had yet to feel any level of success when it came to school or life.

The moment I met Charlie, I knew he had the potential to be something amazing, but I also knew he had no idea he had this potential inside of him. This is where our journey began. I had to get Charlie to see himself the way I saw him, but to do this he had to trust me. I had to gain his trust, so that he could start to see himself through a different lens. He had to believe that he deserved success. To say he didn't trust me in the beginning would be a vast understatement. He was guarded and detached. He tested me with every opportunity he was given. Charlie had very few adults in his life that actually followed through on promises and let their actions speak rather than just words. I told Charlie I would never give up on him and I meant that to my very core. Throughout the years together, Charlie began to see that I meant what I said and I did what I promised. On some days, he would confide in me and give me insights into his life and mindset; he began to see that his past did not define him and that I could accept him for who he was without judgment or ridicule. On other days, he would push me away, shut me down, and close me out, yet my expectations for him never changed and he began to thrive on that consistency of high expectations and unconditional love. Every day was a new day, so no matter how we ended our day together yesterday, I welcomed him with a smile and appreciation. Slowly, Charlie began to experience small amounts of success; finishing an essay, creating a resume. Then the success became bigger; earning credits, having employers calling him to offer him jobs and, ultimately, Charlie graduated from high school in the spring of 2018. Charlie achieved something that two years prior was unattainable, a pipe dream. Today is a new day, and today Charlie can be described as confident, capable, changed.

MANY ADMINISTRATORS AND TEACHERS DO NOT LOOK LIKE OUR STUDENTS

Kat and Charlie were students living lives outside of school unlike my own, or that of my staff. This, in and of itself, is another challenge facing the educational system today, making it more difficult to create connections or better understand the human beings with whom we work. An undeniable fact in our nation is that many administrators and teachers do not look like their students. We often don't come from the same lifestyles or experience the same hardships; we cannot claim the same familial experiences or customs. As a result, we may lack cultural or linguistic competence or can have implicit biases—beliefs or attitudes against a person or group of people of which we are completely unaware. In this instance, first and foremost, we must acknowledge this reality. Michelle Alexander (2012), author of *The New Jim Crow*, notes that, "Decades of cognitive bias research demonstrates that both unconscious and conscious biases lead to discriminatory actions, even when an individual does not want to discriminate" (p. 106). Sometimes this acknowledgment can be as simple as admitting to our students that we may not understand their perspectives or experiences and therefore would appreciate their guidance.

Having this type of awareness schoolwide is imperative as implementation of social, emotional, and academic development (SEAD) philosophies and programs proceed, because such efforts will be ineffective if the potential for bias and discrimination is ignored. In fact, Gregory and Fergus (2017) suggest that "the prevailing understanding of SEL [social and emotional learning] is 'colorblind' and doesn't take power, privilege, and culture into account" (p. 118).

KNOWLEDGE AND AWARENESS ARE POWERFUL ALLIES

We may be hesitant to admit that we, as human beings who have chosen a caring profession, might be inherently prejudiced or discriminatory, but we must take time to consider this possibility. I reflect on the wisdom that can be found in the cliché "You don't know what you don't know." Probably the best guidance a mentor gave me during my first year as an administrator was to "talk less and listen more" as a direct response to this cliché. All professionals, regardless of their role in education, can benefit from this advice. Once in this "listening" state, we can set out to educate ourselves because there is much for us to learn. For example, many people are not aware that

> black youth are two to three times more likely than white youth to be suspended. Similar disparities occur between male and female students; still, in many schools the suspension rate for black female students surpasses the rates for male students who aren't black (Gregory & Fergus, 2017, p. 119).

There is a disproportionality for Latinx students, too, when compared to their non-Latinx white peers. According to Joy Pastan Greenberg (2012), "[Latinx] students have higher retention and suspension/expulsion rates, higher high school dropout rates, and lower completion of college rates that their white counterparts" (p. 75).

And, what about students who are eligible for special education, or those living in poverty—regardless of race, or students who identify as transgender? Studies have found disparities in these subpopulations, and others, as well. Do you think if more educators became aware of the data that expose such disproportionalities, they might be fairer when doling out classroom or administrative discipline? I do. Based on my observations in various school settings, explicit bias—that is, outright and conscious bias—is not prevalent. In fact, I firmly believe that the majority of teachers and administrators do not deliberately choose to show bias, or to be intentionally partial to one student over another, but statistics prove that such bias and partiality happen commonly and consistently (Skiba et al., 2011).

Knowledge and awareness are powerful allies in creating school environments that are inviting, positive, and engaging. Setting schoolwide norms of high expectations that provide opportunities for staff and students to teach each other about cultural and familial customs, to communicate views and needs assertively, and to listen respectfully can contribute to an empathetic school culture, one that promotes genuine acceptance, an appreciation for diversity, and an awareness of situations in which we revert to subconscious biases.

We must also be aware of situations in which we offend, or seem to offend, a student or colleague. Most of us have been in situations in which we felt that we may have offended another person. We may not even be sure of what we did or said to offend; but we can certainly *feel* the aloofness that appears out of nowhere or a new attitude that is discernably different and appears rude or demonstrates without words when we have offended someone. When we sense this, no harm can come from our expressing a sincere apology for anything we may have inadvertently said or done to insult or hurt another. More than once, I have found myself saying something like this to a student, parent, or guardian: "I have a feeling I may have offended you. Please know that this was not my intention. Is there anything you can tell me to help me to be more understanding in the future?" To put oneself on the line in such a way takes vulnerability, but this can be a leadership strength that facilitates a positive outcome. More often than not, the other person offers an explanation and any tension in the room dissipates so that we're able to move forward with clarity and consideration.

WHEN PEOPLE FEEL RESPECTED THEY ARE MORE LIKELY TO ENGAGE

In a similar light, respect—or the lack thereof—can have an impact on our ability to unify or understand each other's perspectives. In my work as a school climate specialist, I spend a great deal of time coaching school leaders and interacting with staff and students. When it comes to respect (which tends to be a school improvement initiative for many schools), more often than not students can tell me that respect *is* a value of the school, but they have difficulty describing what it looks like or defining it because the definition or description of respect can differ depending on our familial culture and traditions, as well as our life experiences. Kids who grow up defensive, or associated with gangs, may see respect as fear, while people who experience family life with an emphasis on old-fashioned values may describe respect as having proper manners or admiration for another. Respect in some cultures requires that you look someone in the eye when speaking, while in other cultures young people show respect to their elders by casting their eyes downward. In a school culture, norms and expectations for respect may need to be identified, established, and reinforced. It is necessary to remedy any confusion around respect in our quest to connect with all stakeholders within our school community. It may be important to identify the need to code-switch by acknowledging the difference between what respect looks like at home and what it looks like at school.

In fact, an inspiring and passionate elementary teacher, Krystal Koontz, uses the analogy of a backpack to help her students think about this issue. She asks her students, "What character traits and behaviors do you need in your backpack at home to demonstrate respect. Now think about this: How does what you put in your backpack in regard to respectful traits and behaviors change for school?" In regard to respect, some of our students need two completely different backpacks.

I notice that when people feel respected they are more likely to engage, interact, listen, and speak up. They are prone to volunteer and are more willing to trust if an air of respect is present. Yet, in order to reach this ideal in a group of diverse people, it is important to agree on what respect looks like within the school community. Because we all come from different perspectives, everyone should have an opportunity to have input in developing a definition or guiding principles for respect. Through surveys, focus groups, and personal interviews, we can gather data in the form of thoughts, views, and perceptions. I have seen schools create exciting celebrations when they reveal the school's new code of respect. And within this celebration is a group of people experiencing camaraderie, unity, and joy.

Keep in mind that it is not measurable objectives, an innovative curriculum, or required testing that leads to this camaraderie, unity, and joy (all of which are essential to a positive school climate). It is the result of people coming together to exchange ideas and engage each other in conversation. If we, as educators, expect to engage our students so that they are excited to learn, if we desire to build productive and collegial relationships with our peers, and if we seek to develop constructive conversations with parents and guardians, then a positive climate based on sincere human relationships and a willingness to understand the perspective of others must come before instruction, training, and assessment.

A concerted effort toward connection with colleagues, as well as a comprehensive program that emphasizes social, emotional, and academic development mindsets and competencies can create a positive school climate and a culture of thoughts and behaviors that contribute to success in school and in life. Throughout this book you will be asked to consider and implement strategies based on a combination of competencies established by the Collaborative for Academic, Social, and Emotional Learning, as well as perspectives and recommendations from the Aspen Institute's National Commission on Social, Emotional, and Academic Development.

TAKE FROM THIS BOOK WHAT WORKS

From the candid viewpoint of my past experience as a teacher and an administrator, as well as my current work as an educational consultant and leadership coach, I find that an open-minded approach, with an analysis and consideration of district or site-based needs, provides for the most effective results. In essence, I encourage you to consider your staff, students, and school community: Take from this book what works for you, and feel free to leave the rest. I do not purport to offer all things to all people. In fact, I have found that such an approach is usually ineffective. However,

I do maintain that if we start with the people, and assess needs from there, we have a better chance for success. After all, when it comes down to what makes an impactful difference, remember: It is always about the people, not the things.

Chapter 1 Study Questions
For Professional Learning Communities, SEAD/SEL Courses, or Book Study Groups

1. What is currently on your plate that causes you to neglect what or who you value? Do you have a person in your life who reminds you to keep your priorities in order? If not, can you think of a person to designate?

2. How do you keep "what's first, first?"

3. What did you notice when you considered who was *not* on your list? Was there a way in which this realization caused in you a desire to refocus your priorities? Please explain.

4. When you considered whose list you might be on, if specific people came to mind, please explain why you would like to be on their lists. What specific actions or ways of being do you practice that would cause another to include you on his or her list?

5. Can you speculate as to who might be on your students' lists? Would their lists be similar to each other? Why or why not?

6. What are your strengths in regard to meeting your colleagues where they are? Do you have any areas of growth or barriers upon which to reflect? Please explain.

7. What do you do to recognize and connect with the student "behind the façade?"

8. Put yourself in the shoes of a student who is asked, "Why did you do that?" or "What were you thinking?" How would you react if a colleague asked you one of those questions?

9. Can you think of a time when it would have been productive to admit to a student that you do not understand his or her perspective or experience and would therefore appreciate guidance?

10. After respect is identified within the classroom, how might you address the need for code-switching (or the need for a separate backpack)?

 Available for download at **resources.corwin.com/StartWithTheHeart**

CHAPTER 2

A Foundation of Love

7 Keys to Connection

Telsche Hipple is a phenomenal teacher! She has a way of connecting with students that is natural, meaningful, and, in my mind, life-changing. I asked Mrs. Hipple to share an example of a student connection that was initially challenging, but ultimately significant, as well as the basis of that connection, to help my readers gain insight from a teacher's perspective. This is her story about a student she refers to as Rees:

Rees was tough. She had an intimidating personality. She came across as knowing what she wanted and how she was going to get it. She had been expelled from school for fighting and she wore it proudly. Rees was not about to let anyone into her personal sphere. As her teacher, I didn't have a strategy other than to let her know that I loved her and I wanted to see her succeed, and maybe even help her realize she didn't have to fight her way through life.

I began to gain Rees's trust a bit as I praised her efforts in her studies and let her know that I was concerned when she wasn't at school. I thought it would help her trust me more if I shared a little bit of my life, which included a challenging time I was presently going through. I told Rees that I was taking care of my mom, with whom I was very close, because she had advancing Alzheimer's. I then got a glimpse into Rees's life at home as she explained that she, too, was very close with her mom. I didn't realize our conversation meant anything to Rees until a few weeks later when she asked if she could work with my mom for her community service project that was required of all of our students. For several days after school the two of them sat together and did crafts. My mom beamed with joy because she loved working with students, and my student's eyes and heart began to soften.

Love, through respect and a genuine interest in Rees's life and education, helped me to chisel some necessary tough spots away to get at the heart of this amazing young woman who was hiding behind a past of hurt, loss, fighting, and betrayal. As a result, I watched her blossom as she began to develop appropriate social skills, respect herself, and achieve academically.

Mrs. Hipple said the positive change she witnessed in this student was based on love. We rarely hear the word *love* used in the context of educational strategies or best practices. In fact, some educators may be tempted to roll their eyes at the presentation of love as a premise for academic success. This may be a natural response, but we know that a correlation exists between connection or building relationships with our students, and academic achievement (Marzano, McNulty, & Waters, 2005; Pianta, 2001). Furthermore, wouldn't you agree that most relationships or connections between human beings are built on love? I'm not referring to romantic love, but this is where most of our minds go when we conjure up the meaning. Perhaps this is why educators hesitate to use the word *love*, at least professionally, that is. Yet the idea that approaching our students and colleagues from a place of love is the cornerstone for connection.

Consider this: If love is the basis for our attitudes and our actions, it is a foundational platform on which to connect with the hearts of others in a promising and productive way. Unfortunately, many people tend to respond to life situations from a place of fear, as opposed to love. The emotion of fear leads to reservation, withdrawal, loneliness, depression, judgment, and anger; these are behaviors that do not foster relationship building, nor do they inspire effective teaching, engaged learning, productive citizens, or the academic achievement that tends to be the ultimate measure of a successful educational mission.

Love, by contrast, does all these things, because it leads to kindness, acceptance, forgiveness, joy, and hope. If given the choice, most would choose love; however, in real-life situations it is often more natural to let fear control our responses. To focus on love, one must be intentional. To do this, we must use *love* as a verb, an action word. Fourteen-year-old Robby Novak, known to many as the Internet sensation Kid President, has articulated this concept quite well in his quest to encourage others to change the world. He says, "[I]t takes one person filled with love and they just have to live it out, and then that person is filled with love . . . and it goes on, and on and on" (Soul Pancake, 2013).

IT MUST START WITHIN

What does it look like to be filled with love and live it out? Well, I have to state the obvious: *It must start within.* If we do not love and care for ourselves, how can we possibly love and care for others? Please take a moment to think about how you choose to show yourself love. Do you take care of yourself? Do you honor yourself enough to carve out time to slow down, relax, and breathe? Do you exercise or meditate? Do you eat well? Do you surround yourself with people who make you better just by being in their presence? Do you think positively of yourself? Do you laugh enough? Do you allow yourself to cry when hurting? These are a few ways to show ourselves love. What do you do? Please jot down your thoughts in this regard (see Figure 2.1).

FIGURE 2.1

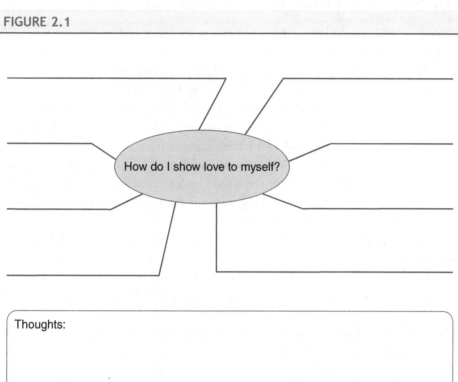

Self-reflection can be challenging, yet it is something that we often ask our students to do, so it is important that we practice it ourselves. More than that, though, when we reflect, we can learn from ourselves and choose to grow. For example, if you had difficulty identifying how you show love for yourself, then you might do well to make some changes in your life. Take time to talk to a friend or family member to get an objective opinion of how you might develop this awareness. At the same time, if ideas flowed easily for you, then you are in a fantastic place to begin to sincerely show others love. In fact, this might come naturally. We show sincere love by practicing respect, offering kindness, and granting forgiveness. We also show love by having high expectations, as well as by providing boundaries, because in doing so we demonstrate that we believe in the ability of others to meet their potential and that, within our care, they will be safe. Finally, although it may seem obvious, once we sincerely and consistently show love, we can begin to use the word *love*. Yes, even in the world of education!

WE SHOWED THEM BY OUR ACTIONS

When I was the administrator for an alternative education high school, every day when my students entered the building and every day on their way out the door, my staff and I would slap high fives, shake hands, and offer fist bumps as we said, "Good morning, we love you. We're glad you're here today!" Or "Good-bye. We love you! See you tomorrow!" Often, too, I would jump on each bus, before they pulled out to take our students home, just to say, "Oh, and, one more thing . . . I love you!" and all of our wonderfully tough, sometimes scarred, always hopeful students would shout back, "We love you too, Mrs. T!" If ever there was a new student, and often there was, he or she would look around the bus, like, "Have you all lost your minds?! Who is this crazy woman? And, did you really say, 'We love you' back?" Inevitably a student would respond with, "I know, right? But just wait, you'll see." And this was said with confidence, because our students did "see" our love every day. We showed them by our actions, and as a result, when we told them we loved them, they believed us. For some of them, hearing and believing that someone loved them happened only at school. Continuing to hear that they were loved, and continuing to see us demonstrate our love by our respecting them, holding them to high expectations, and helping them achieve their goals gave these students permission to begin to love themselves. This is an example of how, as Robby Novak says, love can be "lived out" at school.

Living love can also become real when we simply make an effort to authentically connect with other human beings. Although many of us could say we know "how" to connect with others, I would suggest that we must also then admit that we sometimes get caught up in the demands of our jobs and we tend to forget the little things that help us show others that we care and that they matter. In the world of education today, every one of us, from superintendents to support staff, feels overwhelmed at times. And this feeling doesn't seem to be slowing down or lessening any time soon. Expectations and requirements continue to increase for educators while the amount of time we have to meet these challenges stays the same. Yet we can't lose sight of the human beings who are the students behind test scores or subpopulations, nor those who are staff members behind stacks of papers or ineffective evaluations. We will find more meaning and fulfillment in our vocations when we take just a moment to be human: by greeting students as they arrive at school and using their names while doing so or by stopping a colleague in the hall to check in and say hello. Every act of connecting with the human beings in our midst can relieve our feelings of being overwhelmed, increase student achievement, and improve the general school climate.

7 Keys to Connection

Focusing on the following *7 Keys to Connection* will help you to be conscientious in your efforts to connect:

7 Keys to Connection

1. Stop
2. Look
3. Ask
4. Listen

5. Smile Authentically
6. Connect Kinesthetically
7. Believe Intentionally

STOP, LOOK, ASK, AND LISTEN

Keys 1–4: The first four keys—stop, look, ask, and listen—actually go together. It's imperative that we take time to *stop* when we encounter another person, *look* them in the eye, and *ask,* "How are you?" or any other question . . . and then, *listen* for the answer. Think about it. How many of us use "Hi, how are you?" as a greeting that really just means "Hi"? Almost *ALL* of us!! We walk by someone quickly, say "Hi," how are you?" and we keep walking! We don't really care how they are, or if we do, we are not showing it by our actions, not if we keep walking.

This epiphany came to me when I was forced to slow down a few years ago while enduring intensive treatment for Lyme disease. Normally, I am in "go" mode all of the time. I have so much energy, that I move fast, *and loudly,* everywhere. In fact, a student would often catch me in the hall as I was striding from point a to point b. Said student would say, "Mrs. T, I have a question." And my inevitable response would be, "Walk with me, I have an answer!" And, on we would go!

CLOSE YOUR TABS

It wasn't just my body that moved fast. My mind, too, was on the go. My husband used an analogy once that fit me to a *t.* He said, "Babe, you have too many tabs open." Confused, and likely a bit defensive, I asked what he meant by that. He explained, "Your mind is like a computer with about 20 tabs open at the same time and you keep going back and forth between the tabs. You need to shut it down . . . close your tabs." It was like a lightbulb turned on for me. He was absolutely right! In fact, now, when he can tell that my mind is racing with ideas or things to be done, he will say, "Close your tabs!" It has become an endearing joke, but there is a seriousness about it that I need to take to heart. And although at my husband's urging, I attempted to close my tabs every once in a while, it wasn't until I got so sick, and didn't have the energy to move so fast, that I took time to appreciate the peace that I found in being still. I realized then that it is wonderful that I am filled with energy and enthusiasm, especially as a high school principal. Yet if I don't take time to actually stop long enough to sincerely acknowledge a student, or a colleague, by looking him or her in the eye, with interest and intentional compassion, then my enthusiasm will have no meaning.

So, when you ask someone at school, "How are you?" be sure you stop to listen for the answer. In doing so, you will authentically connect. The same is true of relationships with fellow staff members, family members, colleagues, friends, and neighbors. Taking time to *stop, look, ask,* and *listen* will lead to renewed relationships based on sincerity and intention. By focusing diligently on these four simple words, you can help create a school community and a community in your world outside of work, in which all people feel a sense of belonging based on genuine compassion and interest. Don't expect these four keys to become automatic. Instead, use them as often as you can and be mindful in as many interactions throughout the day as possible. You will begin to see the positive difference in yourself, as well as in those around you. There will be times when you forget and say only, "Hi, how are you?" and then move on without waiting for a response. When you realize what you've done, telling yourself later, "Oops, I didn't stop to listen" or "I had too many tabs open," consider it a step in the learning process. Once you become aware that you're not stopping to listen, but want to, it will be easier the next time to take the action.

SMILING CONTRIBUTES TO HAPPINESS

Key 5: Key 5 is inspired by the Dalai Lama (2013). He suggests that a crucial part of daily living is to smile with genuine affection. If you are conscientious about your smile, it will start in your heart and shine through your eyes. Not only will you feel the difference, but so will the person on the receiving end of your smile. Shawn Achor (2010), author of *The Happiness Advantage,* explains that when people are partnered and one is asked to show absolutely no emotion, while the other is asked to look into his or her partner's eyes and genuinely smile, the person who was to show no emotion invariably smiles. One just can't keep from smiling back. The best part however, according to Achor, is that smiling contributes to happiness. He suggests that, "[s]miling . . . tricks your brain into thinking you're happy, so it starts producing the neurochemicals that actually do make you happy" (p. 206). What a gift it is to connect with others by smiling and, in doing so, creating an opportunity for them, and for you, to experience joy!

MAKE CONTACT AT THE DOORWAY

Key 6: Key 6 may seem contrary to what we continue to hear in the world of education today, but it is important and, thus, should be put into context. We must connect kinesthetically. I realize that, as educators, we are directed continually *not* to touch kids, especially in the realm of special education. Obviously, as professionals, we must respect rules that protect our students, as well their needs for personal space. Furthermore, there may be people with whom we interact in the workplace or community who for religious, cultural, or experiential reasons react negatively to physical touch, and we must respect this response. In this case, if actual touch is out of the question, then use proximity. Touch something that the person you are relating to is also touching, like a desk or chair, anything to demonstrate that connection is important.

At the same time, in most cases, a hand shake, high five, a fist bump, or *some* type of appropriate touch as a greeting or celebration will help you to connect. If every teacher took an extra five minutes to personally greet each student as he or she entered through the classroom doorway with a smile and perhaps a fist bump, it might save instructional time, because the students would feel acknowledged and cared about daily! Many of the classroom management issues teachers deal with on a regular basis have to do with a need for attention. Some students have not received a great deal of positive attention in their lives and therefore will act out negatively with the hope of being noticed. However, if these students are recognized positively at the beginning of every day or class period, you likely can minimize student discipline issues within the classroom, because the students are receiving positive attention immediately.

We are making an important connection when we make contact at the doorway, using this time as an opportunity to smile, look each student in the eye, and perhaps share a quick personal greeting. This effort will start the class period on a positive and encouraging note. It will also allow us to notice if a particular student seems down-and-out sad, ready-to-blow angry, or can't-stay-seated restless, giving us valuable information before proceeding with our interactions and instruction for the day.

FIND SOMETHING, ONE THING, YOU CAN BELIEVE IN

Key 7: Finally, we must believe in our students, as well as our colleagues, intentionally. Intentionality is essential, because often the people with whom we are attempting to connect may not believe in themselves. Find something, one thing, you can believe in about them, and this will help you to connect because, ultimately, it may lead them to believe in themselves, too. As an administrator who worked in alternative education, I interacted with a majority of students who had not been successful in their previous schools. In their own minds, for whatever reason, they saw themselves as failures. So, when our students would say, "I can't," or "There's no way," or "You just don't understand," my staff and I would find something that we could believe in for them. Even if it was initially difficult to come up with a strength, we would take a dominant behavior trait and turn it into something positive. Their stubbornness, for example, we saw as determination, or their anger, as passion. For example, a student who was always arguing to get his point across, would elicit this type of response from a teacher: "Johnny, I love your perseverance. You know what you want and that quality will take you far in life. However, we need to work together on fighting for what you want in a respectful way." When we let our students know that we saw a strength within them, we connect with a small piece of them they didn't even realize existed. Whatever it was we found to believe in, my staff and I would tell our kids, "We believe in you, regardless! So, grab on to our belief, until you can begin to believe in yourself." And, eventually, they did!

I DIDN'T KNOW I WAS SMART

I remember one student in particular, McKayla, an incredibly special young woman. She came to us as at the beginning of her senior year in high school. She had been homeless and had difficulty fitting in at the traditional high school. She was certain that she would not graduate unless she changed schools. From the moment she stepped on our campus, she worked diligently and kept her eye on graduation. And it paid off. As the year drew to a close, McKayla's name rose to the top of the list as the graduating class's valedictorian. I remember calling her into my office with another staff member who was a mentor to her. I was so excited to surprise her with the news and expected her to jump up and down with joy. Instead, she covered her face with her hands as tears rolled down her cheeks. Then she looked at us silently for a moment, her face red and filled with disbelief. She said, "I didn't know I was smart." Our response in unison was, "We did!" We all laughed and celebrated together, and McKayla finally believed.

There may be adults in our lives, too—colleagues, employees, or employers—who struggle with their confidence or sense of self. Paying someone a compliment or verbally recognizing a positive behavior or trait will help a person begin to acknowledge his or her own worth and feel valued by others. It will also open the door to positive communication and genuine connection.

Please take time to consider the 7 Keys to Connection and acknowledge at least one way in which you will make a concerted effort to connect with others in a meaningful way.

The 7 Keys to Connection

With students:

_____

_____

_____

_____

With colleagues:

_____

_____

_____

_____

With friends or family:

_____

_____

_____

_____

With acquaintances or strangers:

_____

_____

_____

_____

When we sincerely connect with others, motivated by our desire to love human beings in a committed and intentional way, we light a spark that helps people begin to experience happiness and believe in themselves. This spark can ignite hope that leads to social, emotional, and academic development.

SOCIAL, EMOTIONAL, AND ACADEMIC DEVELOPMENT—A COMPREHENSIVE PROCESS

So, what exactly is social, emotional, and academic development (SEAD)? It is a comprehensive process by which specific skills and competencies are modeled, taught, and embedded into classroom and schoolwide norms. These noncognitive skills and competencies can include the ability to understand and manage emotions; demonstrate empathy and an appreciation for diversity; establish and maintain relationships; and make responsible decisions, including setting and achieving goals. The Collaborative for Academic, Social, and Emotional Learning (CASEL) created a systemic framework that defines these competencies as self-awareness, self-management, social awareness, relationship skills, and responsible decision making.

According to the Aspen Institute National Commission on Social, Emotional, and Academic Development (2017a), schools have significant influence over SEAD in the realm of understanding, modeling, and teaching necessary skills and behaviors. As such, when social and emotional learning (SEL) is fully integrated into the educational system, it has proven to have a positive effect on academic achievement, graduation outcomes, and workplace readiness.

ACADEMICS AND THE WELL-BEING OF STUDENTS IMPROVE

Researchers from the University of Loyola, Chicago, found that when evidence-based social and emotional learning is programmed properly, both academics and the well-being of students improve (Durlak, Weissberg, Dymnicki, Taylor, & Schellinger, 2011). Their meta-analysis of 213 studies involving more than 270,000 students demonstrated that those who participated in evidence-based SEL programs showed an 11-percentile-point gain in academic achievement compared with those who did not. Students also demonstrated improved attitudes about self and others and positive classroom behavior. Reduced risks for failure were also evidenced by a decrease in conduct problems and emotional distress. Another study found that SEL programs implemented with fidelity can lead to better life outcomes, saving as much as $11 for every one dollar invested on social spending (Belfield et al., 2015). These statistics support district issues and initiatives across the nation: improving test scores, decreasing discipline issues, and improving mental health, all while saving the district money!

In the next five chapters, we will delve deeper into the competencies identified by CASEL, as well as various noncognitive skills, equity considerations, ideas of thought, and practical strategies that correlate with each competency. We will explore social and emotional learning within the context of school climate, academic integration, and explicit instruction. As educators or stakeholders within the school community, we can benefit from learning more about social, emotional, and academic development in our efforts to connect with the hearts of our students and each other as we put love into action.

1. What do you notice about the two hierarchies in Figure 2.2? The Start With the Heart Hierarchy is built on the idea of Maslow's Hierarchy *and* with the understanding that most of our students' safety and physiological needs are met while they are at school. What would be the benefit of embracing a Start With the Heart Hierarchy?

FIGURE 2.2

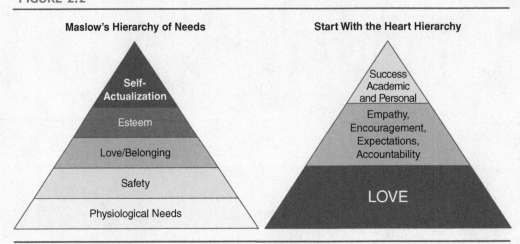

2. How do you "live love" throughout your workday?

3. What was your reaction to the suggestion to connect kinesthetically? What are your beliefs in this regard?

4. What tabs do you have open that hinder you from being emotionally and physically present? Why is it sometimes difficult to close your tabs? At the same time, how does keeping multiple tabs open affect you and those closest to you?

5. Do you have any implicit or explicit biases that might interfere with your ability to believe in your students?

6. How do you acknowledge your belief in your students?

7. What would you feel if you entered a room of colleagues, including your supervisor, and no one acknowledged you? How do you think students feel when the same thing happens to them?

8. Based on the statistics related to social and emotional learning impacting student outcomes, was there a statistic that resonated with you? Please explain.

 Available for download at **resources.corwin.com/StartWithTheHeart**

Self-Awareness

Who Am I? An Essential Question

Who am I? This is a challenging question for adults to answer, let alone kids. But it is an essential question. Earlier in the book, we discussed that what really matters in life is the people, not the things. Furthermore, as people, it is *who we are* that matters, not what we do. People who are self-aware tend to be able to answer the question "Who am I?" more easily. Do you know who you are? I'm not referring to your job title, although this is how we commonly answer the question, as if our profession completely defines us. For example, when I am asked, "Who are you?" it is easy for me to say, "I am a retired principal" or "I am an educational consultant." But those responses do not define *who* I am, they are *what* I do. Don't get me wrong, I chose my vocation purposefully. I do what I do because of who I am. Yet in order to truly understand this and delve deeper into the essence of who I really am, I must assess my emotions and abilities, my sense of self. As we pursue this idea, it might be helpful for you to delve deeper too. If we are going to understand self-awareness in the context of our students, we must be open and willing to connect with our own awareness of self.

Self-awareness is a competency that can be defined as

> the ability to accurately recognize one's own emotions, thoughts, and values and how they influence behavior. The ability to accurately assess one's strengths and limitations, with a well-grounded sense of confidence, optimism, and a "growth mindset" (Collaborative for Academic, Social, and Emotional Learning, 2018).

What Is Really Going on Here?

Recognizing one's emotions; accurately assessing one's strengths and values; practicing self-efficacy; and having a positive, growth mindset are all important components of self-awareness in and of themselves. However, each component is also interrelated and builds on the others. To maintain congruence, our exploration of self-awareness should start with identifying one's emotions, but that's not always easy to do. Emotions can be confusing! Positive emotions tend to be straightforward. If we are excited, eager, or happy, we can usually identify what we are feeling and understand the cause of such emotion. Negative emotions, by contrast, are not so easy to identify. For me, regardless of what I am feeling, if it is negative, my "go to place" is anger. Anger just seems so much easier to deal with than sadness, hopelessness, or desperation. I have difficulty recognizing when I do this. I know that I am angry, I just don't know why, because anger was likely not my original feeling. Fortunately, my husband helps me keep it real. When he asks, "What is really going on here?" it tends to click and I can better identify what I am *really* feeling. And when I actually identify my emotion, the behavior that follows is more thoughtful. For example, if I am sad, but it comes out as mad, I am more likely to initiate an argument with my husband or demonstrate impatience with a student. However, if I take a deep breath, think about what I am actually feeling and why, I am more likely to be more patient with myself, but also with others. In fact, it may even cause me to be more empathetic and understanding.

It reasons that if emotions are challenging for us to identify as adults and professionals, it may be true of our students, as well. If, like me, and maybe you, our students learn to put a name to their emotions, perhaps they'll learn to be more empathetic and understanding too. In turn, this may foster a more positive and accepting class climate and, therefore, improved class management. We know that effective classroom management helps us maximize our instructional time, which benefits all. So, let's pursue this idea of identifying emotions.

With our youngest students, it begins with putting words to feelings. A simple feeling chart can be posted in the room for easy reference to support one-on-one conferencing, class discussions, or writing prompts. Even our youngest learners are familiar with emojis. Printing a poster using various emojis and then working together as a class to determine what feeling or emotion each "face" represents allows students to designate a common class language, and it also provides a reference for individual expression or whole-class problem solving.

If it is necessary to collect data on a particular student's behavior, this idea can be modified so that some of the emojis are listed in a straight line from negative (i.e., angry) to positive (i.e., happy). This can also be done with colors designated to represent various emotions. To operationalize the data, you can place a ruler under the emotion line and convert to inches, or centimeters, the emotion the student chooses on a given day or at a specific time. These data points can be tracked to measure how often a student is experiencing specific emotions. Emojis could also be used in an elementary school classroom during a read aloud, with the teacher using the emoji chart to help students identify how a specific character may be feeling and why.

Provide Students With an Emotional Rating Scale

I have found that older students also benefit from identifying and expressing their emotions. For them, however, it is more about the need for a system that allows them to be as productive as possible as learners. When a student comes into the room carrying a heavy emotional load, his or her open-mindedness to learning may be compromised. The same is true for a teacher. Preoccupation with a burden of mind or heart can negatively influence the teacher's instruction. All members of a class, from the teacher and support staff to the students, need to work together in order for the climate of the classroom to promote engagement, safety, and learning. Yet on any given day, one person in the class may bring an emotion into the room that disrupts the learning of all. I have found it helpful as a teacher and leader to provide students with an emotional rating system that allows them to communicate whether they are having a really good day on an emotional level, or a really bad one. This strategy is based on a continuum of numbers from one to five and serves as a check-in for student to nonverbally communicate if they are in a negative (1) or positive (5) emotional space.

For this strategy to be most effective, emotions that would qualify as negative, positive, or somewhere in the middle must be established. For example, students may brainstorm in small groups or as a whole class to identify emotions that might be identified by the number one. They might suggest that a "1" should indicate feelings such as angry, depressed, hopeless, volatile, or anguish. A "5," by contrast, might be determined to depict emotions such as happy, peaceful, excited, or hopeful. Curious, bored, uncertain, sad, or anxious may fall somewhere in the middle. To put the scale into practice, an administrator, a counselor, or a teacher might say to an individual or a class as a whole, "Show me your number." Students then hold up the number of fingers that indicate their level on the continuum of negative to positive emotional states of being. (It is important, especially when this process is new to students, that they hold their hands close to their chest to promote emotional safety and a more authentic sign. The closer the hand is held to the body, the more likely only the adult requesting the signal will observe the message.)

Like the emoji symbols for younger students, the numerical rating scale provides a common language for older students and also gives them an outlet for emotional worries. I also find it helpful because, without a detailed discussion (which might occur at a more appropriate time), I am able to know at the beginning of the day or class period where I need to show compassion, share excitement, or practice patience. For many students, having the opportunity to acknowledge their feelings without an inquisition or conversation helps them to relax in the knowledge that an adult is aware and cares, which helps them to be more open and willing to take part in class as a responsible student.

At the same time, other class norms should be put into place to provide an opportunity before the end of class for any student who rated their emotional state as a "1" to write to the teacher about it, request time to arrange to see the school counselor or social worker, or make a plan to improve his or her rating. In addition to an awareness of mandatory reporting requirements, there should always be a class system in place that enables students to seek support and guidance if they are feeling low due to a situation that includes neglect, abuse, or any other experience that might lead them to hurt themselves or others.

Who Am I?

When we can recognize and acknowledge our emotions or feelings, we will be more able to have an accurate self-perception, thus allowing us to better answer the "Who am I?" question. The prose in Figure 3.1 was written by a perceptive sixteen-year-old student.

FIGURE 3.1

Who Am I?

I am compassionate. I care about people, the environment, and animals, and I care about the welfare of all of those things. I am motivated now, and I know that I want to be a motivated adult. As much as I hope to change it, I also know that . . .

I am selfish. I wish I could figure out how to be motivated without being selfish.

I am a reader and a writer. I love words and know that behind every word and opinion is someone's own thoughts, judgements, loves, or fears. So really, I am inquisitive.

I am independent. I don't want to be held down by anything in the future. I want to go where I want to go and do what I want to do. I want to see and experience as much as I can, so I know that I have to make choices today that will help me to get there.

But, sometimes, I am a follower. This has gotten me in trouble and it is not who I want to be. It seems weird that I can be independent and a follower at the same time, but I am. So, I guess . . .

I am confused.

Mostly though, I want to be happy. I don't know if it is who I am right now, but it is who I want to be.

—Sarah, 16

This student had the ability and wherewithal to assess her identity. In an effort to understand the thinking process of a student in your classroom, try to do the following exercise as if you *were* a student—but please use the emotions as they pertain to *you*. You can write in any style you choose, but begin with "I am. . . ."

Put Yourself in a Student's Shoes

I am _____

_____

_____

_____

_____

_____

_____

_____

_____

_____

_____

After rereading what you wrote, notice: Were you easily able to identify emotions and/or traits that describe who you are as a person, or did you struggle to identify qualities to explain yourself? Our students fall into both categories. Regardless of age, some of our students know who they are and are able to articulate this with conviction. For others, this exercise is a challenge, but it is an important one because if our students can use words to describe traits or qualities that identify who they are as people, then they will become more self-aware as individuals.

JUST GRAB ON TO MY BELIEF, UNTIL YOU BELIEVE IN YOURSELF

The act of describing oneself is actually an exercise in which we begin to assess (an assessment not connected to test scores, thank goodness!) our individual strengths.

Appraising our strengths in the form of virtues, abilities, and positive character traits contributes a positive awareness of self. Look back to what you just wrote about who you are as a person. Did you notice words you used to describe yourself that might be considered strengths? If so, list them here:

_____

_____

_____

If not, what might that tell you about yourself? Please list at least one lesson learned about yourself by doing this exercise in terms of describing yourself and assessing your personal strengths:

_____

_____

_____

_____

_____

Use this exercise to engage in a conversation with your students. Classroom activities and conversations that encourage students to identify strengths in themselves and each other can help you to create balanced sets for small group learning. These same conversations can also provide opportunities for students to be reflective and may inspire the recognition of a trait or skill that contributes to the betterment of the class as a whole, as well as to self-confidence in the individual.

As teachers and leaders, we need to recognize the strengths, or potential strengths, we see in our students and acknowledge these strengths on a regular basis as a means to improve students' self-perception. Remember McKayla's story from Chapter 2? She had earned the role of school valedictorian, yet she didn't *believe* she was smart. She said she didn't know. For some of our students, we need to believe in them until they begin to believe in themselves. I can't tell you how many times a student has said, "Mrs. T. I can't do it. I just don't have what it takes," and I have responded, "Yes, you do. You may not believe it yet, but I believe. So, you can just grab on to my belief in you, until you believe in yourself." My staff maintained the same philosophy and repeated the same words every time a student expressed doubt in his or her abilities. And with that simple expression of encouragement, eventually, a light goes on in the eyes of a child who lacks total self-confidence. It may be dim at first but can ultimately grow to be bright and strong. One student who stands out in my mind and heart said to his mentor teacher upon graduation, "Thank you. You knew I could do it, even when I didn't. There were so many times I wanted to tell you that you were wrong (and I did!), but look at me now!"

WE PLAY A ROLE IN HELPING OUR STUDENTS DEVELOP STICK-TO-IT-IVENESS

As we recognize the significance of believing in our students in order to foster self-confidence, and telling them over and over of our belief in them, it is important to delineate between self-confidence and self-esteem. In the context of social and emotional learning, *self-confidence* is the capacity to recognize and assert an accurate sense of self. To the contrary, *esteem* is most generally defined as "high regard" with *self-esteem* being a high-regard of self. For decades, research and social movements have promoted empowering children to develop a high self-esteem. Unfortunately, this emphasis on unqualified self-esteem disregards providing children with the ability to develop an accurate perception of self, recognizing and accepting their skill level or prowess at various sports, academic achievements, or levels of talent in the arts. An accurate self-perception provides students with the ability to identify strengths, as well as areas in which they struggle or are challenged. This is the key to self-awareness, and the key to building self-confidence. To be able to identify areas in need of improvement will actually nurture resiliency and promote skills that will enhance a child's life within school, family, and community and help to define the child's identity.

In her book *Grit: The Power of Passion and Perseverance,* Angela Duckworth (2016) explains that:

> Identity influences every aspect of our character, but it has special relevance to grit. Often, the critical gritty-or-not decisions we make—to get up one more time; to stick it out through this miserable, exhausting summer; to run five miles with our teammates when on our own we might only run three— are a matter of identity more than anything else. Often, our passion and perseverance do not spring from a cold, calculating analysis of costs and benefits of alternatives. Rather, the source of our strength is the person we know ourselves to be. (pp. 247–248)

Duckworth brings us back to the "Who am I?" question. We have pursued the answer to this question with acknowledgment of the importance of identifying and recognizing emotions and strengths. Yet, if identity has special relevance to grit, then it is equally important that we play a role in helping our students develop "stick-to-it-iveness," or perseverance, when it comes to frustration, defeat, or discouragement. An accurate sense of self includes an awareness of our personality traits and behaviors that hinder our positive personal growth and deter our likelihood of finding fulfillment or success in school, and in life. Fortunately, school is a natural venue for developing conscientious self-reflection. Within our schools and the climate of our classrooms, we can ask our students to reflect upon personal thoughts, behaviors, or habits in need of improvement.

By simply asking our students to identify a negative emotion or behavior, such as apathy, inflexibility, or opposition, within themselves that tends to impede rather than support them to be productive and effective in their interactions with others and in pursuit of their goals, we empower our students to take action to better themselves. This reflection can, in fact, be the first step in creating positive change. School itself, from the classroom, the lunch room, and recess, to after school clubs and sports, provides ample opportunity to practice improving self-awareness. Just think of the things that might come up: impatience, frustration, negativity, fear, or passivity. Productive class discussions in which norms are established that promote listening and collaborative problem-solving can help students to acknowledge an area in which they desire to improve as well as identify daily opportunities to work on said improvement. For example, if a student is quick to grow frustrated (an emotion), he might be asked to identify what situations trigger this feeling most often and then determine a more positive, constructive response to frustration. Or if a student is inflexible (a behavior), she might be asked to choose between two options that will promote forward movement. These may be limited choices determined by the teacher, ideas suggested by small group discussion to support the student's growth, or notions that are self-determined through a designated reflection period.

It may initially seem that this type of conversation or process will take time away from instruction, but I have found in my own experience in the classroom, and in observations of quality instructional practice, that teachers can gain instructional time by facilitating productive discourse in the realm of self-awareness. Students who are more self-aware tend to be able to better manage their emotions. As we will address in Chapter 4, self-management skills promote effective classroom management and a more positive class climate. Educators know well that classroom management can make or break opportunities for learning, because if a teacher is distracted or interrupted by inappropriate classroom behaviors, then instruction can be delayed, fractured, or convoluted. Hence, when students begin to develop self-awareness—identifying emotions and personality traits, and then choosing options for moving forward—classroom climate becomes more productive and everyone wins.

DISAPPOINTMENT CAN SERVE AS A FACILITATOR OF THOUGHT

Furthermore, students who are aware of their strengths and their areas in need of improvement tend to be more confident and able to demonstrate self-efficacy. According to Albert Bandura (1998), "Perceived self-efficacy is defined as people's beliefs about their capabilities to produce designated levels of performance that exercise influence over events that affect their lives. Self-efficacy beliefs determine how people feel, think, motivate themselves and behave."

A strong sense of self-efficacy can help our students to set and achieve goals, thereby enhancing opportunities for accomplishment and success as learners and, ultimately, as productive citizens. As with any skill development, students become self-aware and develop their self-confidence and self-efficacy at varying rates. Although many of our students achieve self-efficacy with little practice, others take much longer to reach this goal. Some lack the confidence to achieve intended results. Others have difficulty setting goals because they don't have prior experiences with which to connect emotionally. Neuroscientist Mary Helen Immordino-Yang contends that traditional experts supposed that "high-level cognition is purely rational and that emotion comes along and messes it up" (quoted in Varlas, 2018, para. 3). Rather, she suggests, our thoughts are actually controlled by our emotions. Immordino-Yang says, "Emotions drive not just our desire to solve a problem, but also the access to the memory that allows us to make sense of that problem" (Varlas, 2018, para. 5). If our students do not have prior experience with setting and achieving goals, we must provide opportunities for this to take place in our schools.

An experience that helps students to set and achieve goals might be as basic as an all-school reading challenge in which students compete against each other by establishing goals to see who reads the most books in a given amount of time. Practice with goal-setting and achievement can also occur in specific classrooms by asking students to write a personal daily learning goal at the beginning of each class period as an activity starter, and then giving them two minutes at the end of the period to share the goal and their sense or level of accomplishment as a ticket to leave. If they have achieved their goal, they will have a feeling of triumph from which to draw motivation in the future. If they fall short of reaching their goal, they may feel disappointed. But even this disappointment is valuable, as it can serve as a facilitator of thought. Perhaps it will be a catalyst for students to assess and problem-solve how they might find success in meeting their goal the following day.

We Can Encourage Them to Find Their Strengths

The good news is that with self-awareness and self-confidence, self-efficacy can be developed. A phenomenal example of a person who demonstrates such confidence is that of pastor, author, and motivational speaker Nick Vujicic (2018). Nick, who was born without arms or legs, shares a message of hope with audiences across the globe, particularly in schools. He acknowledges that the confidence he has today developed as he grew. In fact, as a child he was depressed and even contemplated suicide. Yet, he had people in his life, including his parents, teachers, and pastors, who encouraged and challenged him. Eventually, he began to believe in himself. He became confident, hopeful, and outgoing. We can be part of that network of support for our students. We can encourage them to find their strengths. Instead of focusing on what they cannot do, we can encourage them to focus on what they can do. Like Nick, when our students can recognize their strengths, they will begin to believe in themselves, and their confidence is likely to grow. Showing a video clip of Nick in action is a great tool to give students an enlightened perspective. According to Landmark School Outreach (2018), "[R]ecent research suggests that by believing you are capable of something, you help yourself on the path to achieving it."

Finally, people with a healthy sense of self-awareness are cognizant of how their emotions, words, and behaviors affect others. I remember seeing a video clip online of a baby elephant who wanted to sit on the lap of a tourist. The elephant nudged her to the ground and then gently (for an elephant, that is) attempted to get as close to her as possible, draping his front legs over her legs and when that wasn't close enough, stretching out across the tourist's body, as she fell back into the mud laughing with joy. This tourist demonstrated the ultimate sense of self-awareness, by being completely in the moment and expressing joy in having such a hysterical encounter. The baby elephant, too, can teach us a valuable lesson. He can remind us of the importance of being well-grounded enough in our own strengths and abilities so as not to intrude on another's beliefs, experiences, or, in the little elephant's case, the human's personal space.

Part of being self-aware is knowing when to be still, be quiet, or step back. Had the tourist expressed fear or anxiety, rather than joy, perhaps the elephant would not have been so indulgent. This is something to remember when we interact with our students as we practice our own awareness skills, but we will also do well to teach this skill, as a way to demonstrate respect for others. Ultimately, increasing self-awareness and practicing skills associated with this competency can be a foundation and extended context for self-management, social awareness, relationship skills, and responsible decision making.

I hope that, as you have read this chapter, you have encountered ideas and reminders that help you to better understand your own sense of self-awareness and the importance of helping our students to understand, develop, and practice the competency of self-awareness. As you think about modeling and teaching this skill, and embedding it into whatever role you serve in working with young people, please consider that the true experts in this field are our students.

While writing this book, I asked students of all ages to share what they would like their principals, teachers, counselors, and anyone who worked with them at school to know about them in regard to each specific social and emotional learning competency. I also asked them to suggest any strategies they felt would be helpful to educators who were teaching these skills in their classrooms or supporting a schoolwide implementation of SEL. I hope you find their insight valuable and applicable to the work that you do in schools.

What You Should Know . . .
Self-Awareness
Straight From the Hearts of Students

- *I know what I feel. I need someone to just listen, hear me out, and when I am done speaking, I will be ready to listen to advice.*

- *I don't try to act mean, but sometimes I do because I don't want you to know that lots of the time, I just don't understand.*

- *I need you to tell me the truth. One thing that I am aware of is that I know when an adult is not being honest.*

- *I know what I am feeling. Don't try to tell me otherwise.*

- *I get embarrassed if I have to read out loud because I know that I am not very good at it.*

- *I am very self-confident, and I need my teachers to understand this and challenge me.*

- *I believe that self-awareness is a personal topic, and I'd have to feel very comfortable with my teacher and class before I'd talk about my feelings.*

- *I personally like to think that I am self-aware and that I understand myself. But I also know that in three years I will look back on myself now and think, "Wow, was I really that naive?"*

- *I am not comfortable showing emotions, so I half-smile when I am happy and have a straight face at everything else.*

- *I am very confident in my school work, but I am uncomfortable when I have to work with others. I'm afraid that I will be left out or that no one will talk to me.*

- *I don't let out my emotions. It scares me. Sometimes I think I will start crying and I won't be able to stop.*

- *I don't think that I am good at anything.*

- *I believe in myself, and I try to tell my friends to believe in themselves too. We all have something we are good at.*

As you read these messages from students, perhaps you could identify a student you know who might have expressed emotions similar to one of those expressed here. If so, with the knowledge you have today or the insight gained from reading these messages, please describe a way you might have changed your interaction with this student or with an entire class in order to help him or her or them to develop the competency of self-awareness:

_____

_____

_____

_____

_____

In addition to students telling us what they want us to know about themselves, they also offer suggestions to help us, as educators, help them to develop and improve their self-awareness skills. As you review the suggestions from students, highlight two or three that resonate with you.

Suggestions From Students . . . Self-Awareness

- Encourage students to be themselves. Let them share what they are good at.

- Be honest with your students, but do it in a way that is kind.

- Try to connect to students on a personal level. Share with them about a time when you felt disappointed, afraid, or unsure, and it will help them to know that it is okay for them to feel that way, too.

- Give students experiences in class where they can step out of their comfort zone. But make it safe by making sure that nobody laughs or puts anybody down.

- Tell students it is okay to fail as long as they try again. You can even give students a chance to do this in class and let them talk about what they learned from failing.

- Always give students opportunities to try new things. It helps them if they can share how it feels to do this. Some of them are afraid or unsure.

- Try to pull students up. Encourage all of them, even if some are a pain in class.

- Provide a little bit of time every day to allow students to just think. Not every student would adjust to this, but for some who maybe feel stress or want to know themselves better, this time would help them to become more self-aware. Then, they could write or share with others about what they were thinking.

- Teach different character traits and ask students which ones they feel are important. Let them talk about what they believe, but make sure everyone listens and is respectful.

- Try to give students real-life examples of why it is important to be self-aware. Show them video clips or play music that they can talk about. They need to know that it is important to know what they feel and what might happen if they don't talk about their emotions. They also need to know how knowing what their strengths and weaknesses are will help them to be better students.

- Make a lesson that lets students show a talent they have or demonstrate a strength, even if it has nothing to do with school. You can still talk about how that skill might help students in their studies.

List below some strategies that you might use to foster the suggestions you high-lighted or to correct a current instructional practice that inhibits the suggestion. If you have difficulty thinking of strategies on your own, use the space below to brainstorm potential strategies with a colleague. You might consider what would be the time–cost benefit or how you might tweak a current lesson to embed one of the suggested strategies.

- *Student suggestion:*

  _____

  _____

  _____

  o *Potential strategy:*

  _____

  _____

  _____

- *Student suggestion:*

  _____

  _____

  _____

  o *Potential strategy:*

  _____

  _____

  _____

- *Student suggestion:*

  _____

  _____

  _____

  _____

- *Potential strategy:*

  _____

  _____

  _____

Thank you for taking the time to process these messages and suggestions from students. Please reflect on this chapter and consider one reminder, new thought, or specific suggestion that resonated for you, personally or professionally. In the specific context you choose (personal or professional), I'd like to conclude this chapter with an opportunity for you to share one behavior, action, or instructional tactic that you will start, one that you will stop, and one that you will continue in regard to self-awareness:

Start, Stop, Continue . . . Self-Awareness

I will START:
I will STOP:
I will CONTINUE:

online resources ⓡ Available for download at **resources.corwin.com/StartWithTheHeart**

Chapter 3 Study Questions
For Professional Learning Communities, SEAD/SEL Courses, or Book Study Groups

1. What do you already do in your classroom or school to model, teach, and reinforce self-awareness?

2. Brainstorm other ways to help students identify emotions other than with an emoji chart or a number rating scale.

3. As educators, we know that one student's emotional state can disrupt the learning of the entire classroom. In your role as an educator, have you ever been the person who disrupted the learning environment? What did you learn from the situation?

4. How might you model and teach self-awareness, and identification of feelings, using an example or story from your life, while keeping it age appropriate and without sharing too much?

5. How do you recognize strengths or potential strengths in your students?

6. Do you have an applicable example of perseverance from your own life that you could share with your students?

7. What would be the benefit of explicitly teaching grit and perseverance at your grade level or within your content area?

8. Where or how might you incorporate reflection into your daily instruction?

9. Rate yourself from 1 (lowest) to 5 (highest) on your awareness of how your emotions, words, and behaviors negatively affect others. Consider your rating and explain anything you would change to increase your self-awareness.

---

online resources ⓡ Available for download at **resources.corwin.com/StartWithTheHeart**

CHAPTER 4

Self-Management

Feeling It, Without Losing It

"Nick, how's it going this morning?" His math teacher asked this question gingerly, because he could tell by the look on Nick's face that today might be one of those days. Nick exploded, "Why are you looking at me? I *hate* when you look at me like that!" and then he stormed out of the classroom. Translation: "I had a really crummy morning, and if you just let me breathe for a minute, I might be all right." It actually took his teacher the first few months of school to learn to translate Nick's language (both verbal and body), but eventually he understood that Nick was not purposely trying to create a scene in class in which his emotions were out of control. Eventually, Nick was able to express that he was embarrassed by this behavior, but he just didn't seem to be able to control it. If something negative happened the night before or in the morning before school, he would start to feel this rage build up in his body, and it didn't take much to trigger an extreme reaction.

Nick's math teacher was perplexed by Nick's outbursts and frustrated when they disrupted the entire class. But he also understood that something more must going on for Nick. So, he mentored Nick. He was patient and kind. He was available after class time to listen when Nick felt inclined to talk. He also sat quietly by Nick's side when talking was the last thing Nick wanted to do. This empathetic and inspired math teacher encouraged and reassured Nick, but he also maintained high expectations for academics and made sure that Nick gave back time, if he chose to leave class to "breathe." He taught Nick how to ask for help, and they developed signals to help communicate when Nick felt like he was losing control of his emotions, so that he wouldn't yell out loud or spew profanities. Ultimately and after various interventions, Nick walked across the stage at graduation! He told his math teacher that it would not have happened without him.

But more telling of the impact this math teacher had on Nick's life was an event that took place in a sushi restaurant nearly a year later. Nick was having dinner with family and friends when his math teacher from high school walked in with his wife. The math teacher saw Nick and, so as not to intrude, gave him a smile and a head nod. Nick smiled and nodded back, both understanding without words that they were happy to see each other. Nick left before his math teacher and wife finished their meal. After dinner, the math teacher asked for the check. The waiter said, "There is no check. The young man who was sitting at the table in the corner paid the bill for you and your wife." The math teacher was touched to the point of tears and grateful to see Nick as a young adult outside of the high school walls who was continuing to learn how to navigate his world and able to express his gratitude.

You Have an Opportunity to Impact the Lives of Your Students

Nick's teacher, Mr. Emm, was a phenomenal math instructor, but what made a life-changing impression on Nick was his qualities as a human being. Mr. Emm knew that Nick could not learn math, or any other subject, if he could not manage his emotions. He realized that although it may have taken an extra minute or so to "check in" with Nick at the beginning of class, the time spent was worthwhile, because it created conditions that allowed Nick to be more willing and able to learn. The fact that this math teacher took time to see the child behind the behavior made an indelible difference in Nick's life. Actually, it made an impact on both of their lives. As an educator, regardless of your role, you have the opportunity to impact the lives of your students—no matter how big your school or how many students in your classroom.

Like Nick's math teacher, we can respond with humanity instead of letting our own emotions get the best of us. Mr. Emm was early in his teaching career, but he was wise. He had the ability to take a deep breath himself, in the midst of Nick's outrageous behavior to ask the question, "What is really going on here?" He didn't take Nick's offensive behavior personally, and he didn't shame or demean him in front of the entire class. Most important, he did not get into a power play with Nick. If you are a teacher reading this book, you may be thinking, "How did he keep his cool? I would have lost it on the kid!" This is reality; it is difficult to keep it together when a single student is disrupting an entire class. Mr. Emm was able to maintain a calm demeanor partly because he had an easygoing and low-key personality. He naturally had strong self-management skills, but he was also not afraid to ask for help when necessary. When this teacher felt at a loss for strategies or ran out of patience with Nick's behavior, he asked colleagues and his supervisor for support and it made a difference, both in how he responded to Nick and in how it helped Nick to learn to self-manage his own behavior.

THE STUDENT COMES BEFORE THE TEST SCORE

Each of us can make a difference, too, regardless of our role in education. It is simply a matter of knowing that the student comes before the test score, that there is more to success than academic achievement, and that academic development is directly related to social and emotional learning. When we consider the whole child, he or she, like Nick, can find victory in school and in life. According to Joshua Starr (2016), who serves on the Council of Distinguished Educators for the Aspen Institute National Commission on Social, Emotional, and Academic Development,

> Those who work in public schools have come to realize that the generation of focus on standardized test scores has narrowed the ability to focus on the "whole child." When I was a central office accountability leader and then a superintendent, I embraced the equity agenda of ensuring all students achieved high academic standards but always felt something was missing. Academic achievement may be necessary, but it's not sufficient. Our challenge as a council is to help the commission understand the direct link between academics and SEL and the practical implications of attending to those "whole child" needs. (para. 3)

Our challenge as educators is to understand this link as well. If we are going to support our students, whose emotions often seem unwieldy and unruly, rather than calm and controlled, we must better understand the competency of self-management. In doing so, we can assess and practice our own self-management skills, in order to determine how best to teach self-management skills independently, as well as apply them as an immersive intervention for all students.

THE WAY IN WHICH STUDENTS RESPOND TO A SITUATION CAN MAKE A DIFFERENCE IN THE OUTCOME

According to Travis Bradberry and Jean Greaves (2009), authors of *Emotional Intelligence 2.0*, "Self-management is your ability to use awareness of your emotions to actively choose what you do and say" (p. 97). Self-awareness is the foundation for self-management skills. The Collaborative for Academic, Social, and Emotional Learning (2018) is more specific in its definition of self-management: "The ability to successfully regulate one's emotions, thoughts, and behaviors in different situations—effectively managing stress, controlling impulses, and motivating oneself. The ability to set and work toward personal and academic goals."

The skill of managing one's emotions, so that they facilitate positive outcomes rather than hindering them, is a functional aptitude that promotes productivity and effectiveness in one's personal, educational, or professional life. In regard to students, Antwan Wilson, former chancellor of the Washington, D.C., public schools, says, "Too often students who aren't successful, fixate on what's happening *to* them. We want students to understand that they play a role. Did you study, did you read, did you do your homework?" (Aspen Institute National Commission on Social, Emotional, and Academic Development, 2017b). It is crucial to help students, regardless of their age, know that the way in which they respond to a situation can make a difference in the outcome. For example, if a student receives an F on an assignment, and is disappointed when the paper is returned, she is more likely to receive an explanation for the grade, as well as potential opportunities to improve, if she calmly requests a time to talk with the teacher about her grade. Conversely, if the student screams profanities, blames the teacher, or stalks out of the class, she is apt to set herself up to be sent to the office to see an administrator for being disrespectful. As a result, the student not only has an F, but she also has a discipline referral and potential consequences.

If We Take Time to Think in Alignment With Our Belief System, We Can Assert Control

So how do we help our students learn to control their impulses? Is it as simple as teaching them to take a moment to breathe before they express themselves? In many cases it can be, but sometimes it takes a more intentional effort. To better control our impulses, we benefit from recognizing that subconscious negligence can lead to impaired self-management. Years ago, as a ninth-grade health teacher, I asked our school counselor to come in to talk with my students about alleviating stress. She drew a diagram on the board (see Figure 4.1). In it she simplified a complex model from the work of Albert Ellis, on rational emotive theory.

The school counselor went on to explain that when there is an activating situation that is completely out of our control (A), our response to that situation can lead to potential consequences (C) causing stress, instability, and irrationality, because we let our emotions prevail. For example, if a ninth-grade student observes his girlfriend whispering and laughing with another boy (who happens to be his best friend), he may get jealous, explode, and confront the boy with a right hook. As a result, he potentially ruins a friendship, jeopardizes his relationship with his girlfriend, and gets suspended for fighting. He went right from A to C.

FIGURE 4.1

A ————————————————————→ C
(Situation or Activating Event)   (Potential Consequences)

Most of us, as occasionally irrational and emotionally inspired humans, adults and students alike, tend to neglect B (see Figure 4.2). Can you surmise what B represents?

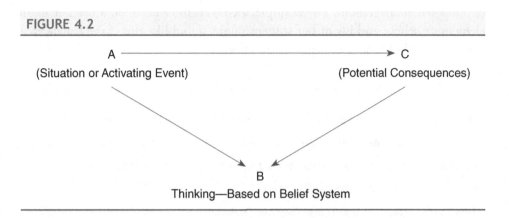

FIGURE 4.2

A ————————————————————→ C
(Situation or Activating Event)   (Potential Consequences)

B
Thinking—Based on Belief System

Thinking! We seldom take time to think when we are feeling frustrated, angry, sad, jealous, or any other negative emotion. When we don't think first, we are more likely to experience emotional stress or upheaval because an outcome that might be more positive in the presence of impulse control ends up as negative. We may not be able to control the situation, but if we take time to *think* in alignment with our belief system, we can assert control and potentially experience a more positive outcome. In our example, if the ninth-grade student observed his girlfriend whispering and laughing with his best friend, he could have thought to himself, "I don't like how that looks, but I trust my girlfriend, so I need to ask her." Then, he asks her and she replies, "You don't have to worry, but I can't tell you what we were talking about because your birthday is next week and I don't want to spoil the surprise." Ultimately, the boy sighs with relief, knowing that his girlfriend and best friend are planning something for his birthday because they care about him. No bruised hand, damaged relationship, or time spent with the principal.

CAN YOU TELL ME MORE?

Sometimes we just need to remember to *think*, even though it might not be our most immediate response. Thinking in a way that leads to a more positive outcome actually has a great deal to do with the questions we ask. We can help our students experience more constructive and encouraging outcomes by asking questions that lead them to be proactive in their thinking. Examples of such questions include the following: Can you tell me more of what you are feeling right now? What do you think the other person may be thinking or feeling? What might you *do* to create a more positive outcome in this situation? You will find it amazing to engage in a conversation with a student based on these questions. Rather than being defensive or defiant, students are likely to be introspective and thoughtful. Keep in mind, however, that you have a small window in which to ask these questions to ensure they will have a positive impact on the immediate situation. Thinking through prospective situations in which these questions might be asked ahead of time will help you when the situation arises, giving you an opportunity to help your students develop self-management. For example, a conversation between a teacher in an elementary school and his or her student might sound like this if the teacher has thought ahead of time about specific questions to ask:

Teacher:	Beth, can you tell me more about why you blurt answers?
Student:	I get excited because I know the answer and I can't wait to tell.
Teacher:	What do you notice in your classmates when you blurt answers?
Student:	They act like they're mad.
Teacher:	What do you think they are feeling?
Student:	Maybe they're frustrated because they know the answer too?
Teacher:	What step could you take to practice self-discipline so that you don't blurt as often?
Student:	I don't know.
Teacher:	What do you think might happen if you tried to write your answer as soon as you think of it, and then raise your hand so I can call on you?
Student:	Maybe if I write it down right away, I won't blurt out.
Teacher:	I think you could be right. I know it will take practice, but it could be better for you and the other students in class. If you are successful, how do you think they might feel? And, how might you feel?

The questions that lead to these types of courageous conversations can promote well-being and foster a more positive learning environment if they take place with kindness and sincerity. Can you reflect on a specific situation in which a student *reacted* without thinking and it led to a negative outcome? What questions might you have asked that student to help him or her realize the chance for a more positive outcome?

The Chance for a More Positive Outcome

Specific situation:

_____

_____

_____

Negative outcome:

_____

_____

_____

Potential questions (from you):

_____

_____

_____

Potential answers (from student):

_____

_____

_____

_____

More positive outcome (describe what it could have looked like):

_____

_____

_____

_____

WE CAN ASK THEM TO NOTICE WHAT THEY ARE THINKING AND FEELING

Asking ourselves or others questions that stimulate productive thought takes intentional effort, but it is an endeavor that might be easily established as a norm for classroom behavior. When it becomes a routine in the classroom, it converts to a tool or strategy that students can use on the playground, in the cafeteria, on the bus, and at sporting events. Eventually students might apply this process to their lives at home and in the community. In doing so, healthy self-management skills will prevail in the form of productive impulse control. Other strategies for developing or improving self-control that can transfer from school to the classroom are mindfulness through noticing and guided meditation, flexible seating, and the use of movement.

Mindfulness is the act of noticing one's thoughts, feelings, and body sensations to enable conscientious response. When students appear frustrated or agitated, we can ask them to notice what they are thinking and feeling. In doing so, we help them to manage their responses. Creating a safe space or peace corner in every classroom can teach students how to reflect and self-regulate as early as kindergarten or first grade. Guided meditations also foster mindfulness and can easily be found online for student groups. I have spoken to elementary and secondary teachers who consistently use guided meditation for just a moment or two at the beginning of each day or class period to help students to focus and calm themselves. Every one of these teachers has found the process to be valuable in helping students to better control their behavior. Making flexible seating an option for some students also promotes improved self-management. A ball chair, balance stool, or standing desk may enable a student who moves incessantly to focus more readily on a lesson. Finally, students of all ages struggle when required to sit still for extended periods of time. A program like *Move It* (The PE Geek Apps, 2018) can be implemented intermittently throughout a class period for just 60 seconds, and will help students to be more focused and productive. These are just a few of many best practices in social and emotional learning that support the development and improvement of self-control and decrease inappropriate behaviors or impulses.

At the same time, we cannot disregard the fact that some students may need more specific intervention to help with impulse control. For medically diagnosed concerns such as attention-deficit/hyperactivity disorder or oppositional defiant disorder, medication or individual guided strategies may be in order. A school social worker or counselor might work with the student's family and doctors to design a plan to support self-management skills and reduce inappropriate impulses, destructive compulsions, or negative outbursts.

Choose to Be Respectful

Helping students to recognize their emotions and then control them when things don't go their way takes self-discipline, which is an essential self-management skill. Brian Tracy (2011), author of *No Excuses! The Power of Self-Discipline,* presents this definition from Elbert Hubbard: "Self-discipline is the ability to make yourself do what you should do when you should do it, whether you feel like it or not" (p. 7). I love this definition because by referencing what one should do (and I typically advocate against "shoulding" on ourselves), it indicates that self-discipline requires us to consider what is right and wrong. Sometimes it takes self-discipline to be kind, but it is the right and good thing to do, regardless of the behavior displayed by the person to whom kindness is offered. We can teach our students to practice self-discipline when responding to another who is being disrespectful. A typical student reaction is to meet disrespect with disrespect. How often have you heard a student say, "I'm not respecting 'so and so' because he doesn't respect me." We can teach our students that when they let someone else's behavior determine their own, they give away all of their control and power. By our actions and our instruction, our students will understand that a person who has self-discipline can *choose* to be respectful regardless of how another person is behaving. Thomas Jefferson once said, "Sir, I will treat you like a gentleman, not because you are one, but because I am" (Character Counts!, 2017). If we help our students to recognize self-discipline as a choice, we can help them feel empowered to do right, to be kind, and to honor themselves and others.

To help our students notice the benefits of self-discipline, we can ask them to create a bubble map reflecting on positive experiences or outcomes that can be a result of practicing self-discipline. Tell your students that there are no right or wrong answers for this exercise. It is meant strictly as a reflection opportunity to increase their awareness of the benefits of self-discipline. Fill out the bubble map shown in Figure 4.3 to use as a potential example for your students.

FIGURE 4.3   Possible Positive Outcomes of Practicing Self-Discipline

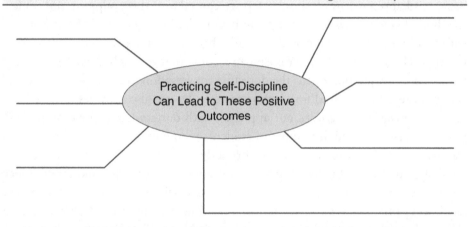

Practicing Self-Discipline Can Lead to These Positive Outcomes

After this activity, help students engage in productive conversations by asking questions such as, "What did you learn from this exercise?" and "What did you notice or realize about the control you have over your choices to practice self-discipline?"

Renowned UCLA basketball coach John Wooden was known for encouraging his athletes to discipline themselves so that others didn't have to. Coach Wooden compelled the young men under his tutelage to understand that "[w]hen you lose control of your emotions, when your self-discipline breaks down, your judgement and common sense suffer. How can you perform at your best when you are using poor judgement?" (Wooden & Jamison, 1997, p. 183). Sometimes when our students do not receive immediate feedback or gratification, they lose control of their emotions. As educators, we can encourage our students to practice self-discipline as an opportunity to learn. Lessons of patience, perseverance, and fortitude can be found in practicing self-restraint and will power.

What About This Situation Is Within My Control?

Some of our students struggle with self-management due to adverse childhood experiences (ACEs) that can result in social, emotional, and cognitive impairments. In fact, according to the Centers for Disease Control and Prevention (2016), the higher the number of ACEs a child has (ACE score), the greater the chance that the child will experience negative long-term effects. As educators, we must be cognizant of this fact because safe, stable, and nurturing environments can help. If our students come from a place of trauma, they may be more prone to stress, behavior issues, and absenteeism. A simple step we can take to show support and understanding of students who are struggling is to replace the question "What is wrong with you?" with "What happened to you?" This question may be more appropriate for high school students. It isn't meant to assume that every child has experienced trauma, but the question opens the door to a conversation that may lead the school system to recognize a need for support services. Its use also provides us, as educators, with insight that guides our approach with our students. For example, if a particular class has a high number of students who have experienced adversity or trauma, we may be more inclined to incorporate stress management techniques into the daily routines of our classrooms. In addition to using the techniques of guided meditation, movement, and breathing, we can also help students to reduce stress by facilitating problem-solving scenarios. Teaching students to ask questions like, "What about this situation is within my control?" or "What about this situation is out of my control?" empowers them and provides them with an opportunity to manage a portion of their lives in a positive way, and to let go of that over which they have no control. These questions are most effective when we provide an opportunity for conversations and brainstorming that are relevant to our students' lives.

I realize these conversations take time, time you often don't have, so consider having a one-on-one discussion outside of class time or when the rest of the class is engaged in another activity. Also, in an effort to make the best use of class time and interweave this life skill into academics, you might facilitate small group discussions to brainstorm solutions for content area issues using these questions. In a math class, a discussion might involve asking students to notice what type of math problem causes the most frustration for each student. Having various students brainstorm and demonstrate ways to work the problem that help them to control their emotions while solving it could benefit all students in the small group. Every student will likely walk away having learned at least one coping strategy and one new way to solve a math problem. Sometimes peers are the best teachers; we can serve as effective facilitators if we suggest or guide the questions.

When our students learn ways to reduce their stress and begin to actively practice self-discipline, they are more likely to be self-motivated and able to set and achieve goals, the final components of self-management we will discuss in this chapter. Self-motivation is an intrinsic quality for many individuals. They may be competitive with themselves and others and therefore find fulfillment in completing tasks and accomplishing goals. Other people may find self-motivation elusive or outright nonexistent, but that does not mean that it can't be developed.

OUR EMOTIONS ACTUALLY STIMULATE SELF-MOTIVATION

In an article written for *Time* magazine, Kevin Barker (2014) suggests that "[w]e need to think to plan, but we need to feel to act." Our emotions actually stimulate self-motivation. It may seem ironic that self-motivation is often triggered by something outside of ourselves. Consider the following concepts as potential catalysts to help your students develop motivation within themselves:

- *Failure is a great motivator.* Fortunately, this concept is gaining renewed appreciation through social and emotional learning philosophies. For years, parents (and teachers) did not let children fail because they did not want to negatively impact self-esteem. By preventing opportunities for failure, we prevented opportunities for growth, problem solving, and the amazing feeling that occurs after finally figuring something out or succeeding in learning a new skill. Think about it: Most adults likely remember the feeling of riding a two-wheel bike for the first time. You tried and tried, until you finally maintained your balance and pedaled yourself through the wind. Prior to that you might have scraped your knees, bruised your elbows, and had to brush the dirt from your hands after tumbling to the ground. It was these initial failures to ride a bike independently that made the eventual success of riding a bike alone so thrilling. The memory of this feeling likely motivates us to try something else that may be new or unknown. However, many children today do not experience this. Think about the bike example. Today there are "no-pedal balance bikes" that allow a two-year-old to get the feeling of riding a bike. It is a phenomenal invention for balance and it expedites the task of learning to ride a bike, but it can eliminate the motivation that comes from failure and the emotion connected with this experience.

- *Relationships influence motivation.* Building trustworthy relationships with our students can influence levels of motivation. For example, if I have built a trusting relationship with a student like McKayla (see Chapters 2 and 3), and I have demonstrated my belief in her efforts, she may be motivated to attempt a new skill based on my belief in her or because she values our relationship and doesn't want to disappoint me.

- *Release of "happy" chemicals in our brain serve to internally produce motivation.* Dopamine, serotonin, and oxytocin are released by the brain in response to thinking positively or receiving positive encouragement from another human being. This is why it is so important for us to encourage our students and find something positive in them in which to believe. This is also why it is important that we teach our students to focus on positivity. If they *feel* good, they are more likely to be motivated to engage, explore, and achieve.

- *Storytelling evokes emotions that inspire motivation.* Sharing stories makes *others feel*. When we feel, we act (Barker, 2014). So, tell your students stories. Help them to invest in the plight of others. Compare journeys and encourage application to personal life situations. At the same time, we must be attentive listeners because sometimes our students will have stories of their own to tell.

- *Accountability motivates.* Verbalizing a desire to try something new, accomplish a goal, or complete a task adds an element of accountability that motivates us to do what we say we are going to do. You might argue that this is not *self*-motivation, and I agree. But I also suggest that accountability can be the catalyst for self-motivation. An example is a commitment to exercise. If I make a deal with myself to exercise daily, but tell no one, then there are no outward consequences (other than my level of fitness) to motivate me. But if I tell someone, I am more likely to follow through because this person may ask me about what I did for exercise, encourage me when I procrastinate, or celebrate with me when I experience positive results. In this way, accountability tends to make our commitments to tasks, goals, or experiments more real. So, provide opportunities in class for your students to respectfully keep each other accountable. Arrange for students to interact with accountability partners. They might share the results of their positive behavior logs, homework completion, or any goal to which they have committed.

Does one of these ideas for helping students become motivated stand out to you? Please choose one and explain how you might incorporate it into your class routine:

_____

_____

_____

_____

_____

Refer back to Nick's story at the beginning of this chapter. How do you think the various components of the self-management competency would have helped you to deal with Nick's behavior if you were his teacher? Or, have you learned any ideas or gained insight regarding how you might help a student like Nick to develop or improve his self-management skills? Please share any reflections that occur to you:

_____

_____

_____

_____

_____

In the boxes that follow, you'll hear from students sharing what they think you should know about self-management and their suggestions for teaching the competency.

What You Should Know . . . Self-Management

Straight From the Hearts of Students

- *Sometimes I can feel my emotions raging, and I don't know how I will react. It kinda scares me.*

- *Sometimes it is easier to practice self-control or manage my emotions than at other times. So, it is okay to ask me if you can help.*

- *I want my teachers to notice if my behavior changes and ask if I am okay, like my friends do.*

- *I have issues with my behavior and learning. I just need someone to take time and work with me.*

- *If you see my emotions getting in the way of my work, I want you to talk to me.*

- *I'm very emotional when I'm stressed. But honestly, sometimes I need you to just let me suffer. Eventually, I'll calm down and manage to do my work.*

- *When I handle my emotions and behaviors, sometimes it is really hard, but other times I can handle them really well. It helps if you notice this.*

- *If you need to talk to my parents, please tell me. Sometimes I get in bad trouble at home. Maybe tell them something good.*

- *If my teacher is someone that I feel comfortable talking to, I can usually get a better grasp*

(Continued)

(Continued)

on my emotions. But, if I know that my teacher won't talk to me or understand, I can get out of control.

- I can get pretty mad, pretty quick. If you notice this and back off for a minute, it helps.

- I have a job after school and a baby brother I have to watch. It gets to be too much for me to handle.

- I'm still learning what it means to be responsible, and I seem to mess up a lot. At least that is what my parents say.

- Remember that we are kids. Sometimes just let us be kids.

- I get mad when a teacher accuses me of something I didn't do. I wish you would ask me before you make assumptions.

- In order for me to manage my emotions, I have to draw or paint to get my feelings out.

- I manage my emotions by suppressing them and turning them off. So, if I look emotionless, then something is wrong.

- I am constantly stressed out. I try to be perfect, but it doesn't work.

- Sometimes I don't even know what I feel. I just need support.

As you've done in previous exercises, please identify a student you know who might have expressed emotions similar to one of those expressed in the "What You Should Know" box. With the knowledge you have today or the insight gained from reading these messages, please describe a way you might have changed your interaction with this student or with an entire class in order to help him or her or them to develop the competency of self-management:

_____

_____

_____

_____

_____

Here are suggestions from students to help us, as educators, help them to develop and improve their self-management skills. As you review the suggestions, highlight two or three that resonate with you.

Suggestions From Students . . . Self-Management

- Be patient, because not all kids have self-management skills.

- Please take time to ask students what they are thinking or what is wrong.

- Teach students skills to help them calm down, like counting to ten or taking a breath before they say what they are thinking out loud.

- Ask students how they are every day, and be sincere about it.

- Develop relationships with your students so that you can tell if something is wrong or if they are upset.

- Don't only teach your students to self-manage. Teach them in what situations it is okay not to. Like, teach them that crying is okay. Teach them that people might take advantage of them if they cry, but that doesn't mean that they should never do it.

- Sometimes it is important to give students space.

- Give students time in class to set goals to get their work complete. And if you haven't already done it, actually teach them why setting goals is important.

- Try to make class fun. It helps students who get in trouble often to behave because they don't want to miss out. This is also good so that the students who are grumpy can be happy.

- Do activities in class that help students express and control their emotions, like fun competitions or challenges.

- Don't say something to embarrass a student in front of the whole class. That is when students most often lose it.

- Homework stresses students out, so make sure it is meaningful. Don't just pile on the work to make the class hard.

- Don't jump to conclusions.

- Don't tell students that their emotions are wrong. Just help them to recognize when an emotion causes them to behave in a way that gets them in trouble.

- Meditation can help.

- Let students leave class if they're really upset. If it is me, sometimes I just need a minute, but other times I really need to go to the counselor.

(Continued)

(Continued)

- Teachers should give students a chance to get their feelings out by doing different types of activities like physical exercise or art.

- Be kind to *all* students.

- Empathize with students. Sometimes if you try to understand what is going on with them, they won't act like jerks.

- Make it clear that you are there for your students, even though your main job is to teach. And if you don't want to be there for your students, then teaching might not be good for you because students need their teachers.

Please list below some strategies that you might use to foster the highlighted suggestions or to correct current instructional practices that inhibit them. Don't forget to brainstorm potential strategies with a colleague if you have difficulty thinking of strategies on your own.

- *Student suggestion:*

  _____

  _____

  _____

  ○ *Potential strategy:*

  _____

  _____

  _____

- *Student suggestion:*

  _____

  _____

  _____

  ○ *Potential strategy:*

  _____

  _____

  _____

- *Student suggestion:*

  _____

  _____

  _____

○ *Potential strategy:*

  _____

  _____

  _____

As we conclude this chapter, please share one behavior, action, or instructional tactic that you will start, one that you will stop, and one that you will continue in regard to self-management:

Start, Stop, Continue . . . Self-Management

I will START:

I will STOP:

I will CONTINUE:

1. What is your personal philosophy regarding "putting the student before the test score?" Do your instructional strategies and classroom environment align with your philosophy? Please explain.

2. Consider Figure 4.2, which represents a modified version of the rational emotive theory. Please explain a way in which you can integrate this model into instruction with application to your grade-level or content area.

3. Can you think of an interaction between you and a student or colleague that escalated into negative words or behavior? How might it have looked different if you asked the question "Can you tell me more…?" at the beginning of the conversation?

4. Can you think of a time when you chose to be respectful to a student or colleague, even though it was challenging? Without using names or identifying information, what did it look like? How did it feel?

5. Think about John Wooden's quote: "How can you perform at your best when you are using poor judgement?" Can this be applied to educators? If so, what is a potential result of losing control of our emotions in a way that affects our judgment and common sense?

6. Is there a situation within your professional life with which you are currently dealing that would benefit from you answering the question "What within this situation is within my control?"

7. Can you describe a situation in which accountability motivates you personally or professionally? How might you share, teach, and/or model accountability for your students using your situation as an example?

---

online resources ⏷ Available for download at **resources.corwin.com/StartWithTheHeart**

CHAPTER 5

Social Awareness

Seeing From the Inside Out

In the fifth grade, my sister, Kelly, was given a nickname by a sixth-grade boy, Richard, who liked to make fun of her. He called her "Green Martian" as if it was her name, with judgment and disdain. I knew his words hurt her feelings, but she didn't let it show. I, on the other hand, as the scrawniest girl in the fourth grade, wanted to tackle Richard and punch him in the nose. But I followed Kelly's lead instead. Even though he teased her, actually bullied her by today's standards, she always treated him with dignity and respect. How she had the wherewithal to do that as a child, I just don't know. As I look back now, I think she knew that Richard, really, was just socially unaware. He didn't know my sister for who she was on the inside, and as a result he missed out on the joy of who she was as a human being. He judged her by what he saw: a little girl who was green. Yes, green . . . in the literal sense. You see, Kelly was born with a liver disease called biliary atresia. It caused her skin to be incredibly jaundiced because her bile ducts were blocked and her bilirubin levels were so high. Her stomach was also extremely distended because her liver was so swollen in her little body. So, Richard teased her because of how she looked on the outside. Other students who knew Kelly for who she was on the inside saw beyond the way she looked and experienced her kindness, intelligence, and sense of humor. In fact, Kelly had a giggle that was just contagious, so there was a lot of laughter in Kelly's friendship circle.

I was only ten when Kelly passed away at the beginning of her sixth-grade year. Richard had gone on to seventh grade by then and may have forgotten all about her. But after Kelly died, I thought of Richard often. I wondered if he knew what he was missing by teasing Kelly the way he did. He missed out on the loyalty she showed her friends, the laughter she created in a room full of people, and the creativity she inspired by her curiosity. His perspective was so limited that it prevented him from learning and growing as an individual. I believe that had Richard seen Kelly for who she was on the inside, his life would have been fuller.

UNDERSTAND THE POWER OF PERSPECTIVE

As educators, isn't that what we want for our students? We want them to have full lives: full of learning, yes, but also of love, acceptance, and the life lessons that come from appreciating another's perspective or diversity. In fact, the competency of social awareness is intended to help our students experience all that life has to offer by understanding and appreciating humanity in its all-encompassing uniqueness. The Collaborative for Academic, Social, and Emotional Learning (CASEL; 2018) defines social awareness as "[t]he ability to take the perspective of and empathize with others, including those from diverse backgrounds and cultures. The ability to understand social and ethical norms for behavior and to recognize family, school, and community resources and supports."

Throughout this chapter we will explore various components of social awareness as defined by CASEL: perspective taking, respect for others, empathy, and appreciation of diversity. We will also pursue the idea of cultural humility in the context of social awareness. There are various strategies to help our students develop, practice, and experience social awareness. It starts by enabling our students to understand the power of perspective. We know we are all different. Our individual life experiences determine our perspectives, or our points of view, and our attitudes toward people and things. Our students will develop social awareness when they begin to understand and respect that people have different perspectives based on what they have experienced: how they were raised, what their parents taught them, what customs they have practiced, what opportunities they have encountered, and what challenges they have overcome.

INDIVIDUAL PERSPECTIVES ABOUT LIFE AND PERSONAL EXPERIENCES CAN BE A VALUABLE LESSON TO ALL

Perspective taking is a term commonly used among experts in social and emotional learning and is defined in its simplest form as "the ability to see things from another's viewpoint" (Fields & Fields, 2010). When we begin to help students develop social awareness, specifically perspective taking, we must remember that our students are the experts on their own life experiences. They know best their feelings, experiences, challenges, and hopes. Giving our students the opportunity to share their individual perspectives about life and personal experiences can be a valuable lesson to all. However, this will happen only if the educator has created an environment in which it is safe to share, question, and listen.

One suggested activity that fosters this kind of environment is group sharing. Teachers might ask students to bring in items that represent their culture, traditions, or a special family experience as one way to help a group of students begin to appreciate one another's perspectives. These items can be shared within small groups, and then students can express in writing or share with the whole class one new custom they have learned from another person that demonstrates appreciation for differences. The same can be done with talents or challenges. I know the students in my sister's fifth-grade class loved and appreciated her because her teacher created an environment in which Kelly was able to share not only about hospital visits and yucky medicine, but also about the fun that she had with her family, her love of her pets, and her positive spirit. All of the students may not have understood what it was like for Kelly to live with a liver disease, but many could identify with her love of animals or the experience of having to take a medicine that tasted horrible. This gave them a common ground that became the foundation of open minds and hearts as they came to appreciate those things that were different in their lives.

Using common ground to provide an avenue for perspective taking can be a conduit for teaching social awareness. Kadhir Rajagopal (2011), or Dr. Raja as he is known to his students, was a math teacher who positively impacted the lives of his students, many of whom were African American and Latino students from low-income urban areas. In his book *Create Success!* he says,

> I don't teach by race. I teach to their collective culture. I find what appeals to most of my students—that I am also comfortable using—and then exploit these commonalities. Any teacher can do this. Any teacher of any race or gender has something in common with or can find something that relates to most of his or her students. Remember, though: Put it in their language, but don't come off as fake. (p. 295)

Perspective taking, as a component of social awareness, can also be taught by using visual images that present opportunities for discussion and growth. An image like the one in Figure 5.1 can facilitate discussion about viewing a situation through a different perspective, whether in regard to human beings or in regard to an academic challenge. For example, knowing there is likely more than one way to solve a math problem enables students to understand that there is more than one way to understand or experience family, traditions, language, or culture. Such lessons learned in the classroom can effectively be transferred to understanding various perspectives in life.

FIGURE 5.1

SOURCE: iStock.com/tintin75

WE MUST BE ABLE TO HAVE AND DEMONSTRATE RESPECT FOR OTHERS

To engage in productive conversations that seek to understand another person's or group of peoples' viewpoint or perspective, we must be able to have and demonstrate respect for others. This is another component of social awareness. As I mentioned in Chapter 1, when I am working with schools on developing a positive school climate, I have learned that most students and school staff can tell me that respect is important, but they differ in their understanding of what respect means or looks like. Whether through a whole-school survey that includes all stakeholders or an in-class discussion with a small group, it is important to develop a definition and vision for respect. We can ask questions as a prompt for class discussions, writing assignments, or partner dialogue. Sample questions might include the following:

- What does respect look like to you?

- How does being respectful in a stressful situation lead to a positive outcome?

- What would be the benefits of acting in a respectful way to adults?

- How can respect help our school?

- How might it help you if you practice respect at home?

- What effect can disrespectful behavior in the classroom have on the students in that class?

- If all students in class practice respect, what will the class look like?

When we agree on a definition, we can incorporate expectations for respect into our classroom culture and reinforce respectful behavior among our students. This type of class discussion also may present the ideal time to address the importance of self-respect with students. Self-respect is a crucial trait that helps young people to be assertive, make responsible choices, and be respectful of others. Again, however, we need to help students understand that having self-respect is not the same as having self-esteem. If students have just discussed what respect looks like in the context of a classroom or school in general, they should be able to extend the lesson by answering the question "What does it look like to respect yourself" or "Why is it important to respect yourself?"

USE SCENARIOS

Once a common definition of respect is in place, role-playing can be an enjoyable strategy for teaching elementary students respect of self or others, whereas brainstorming respectful behavior for given scenarios is a fun activity for secondary students. Feel free to use these scenarios with your students:

- Malik feels that his teacher treated him in a disrespectful way in front of the class. How might he express his feelings to her in way that is respectful?

- Carline was accused of stealing money from Daniella. Daniella confronted Carline with this accusation in front of the entire lunch table. Carline has no idea why Daniella suspects her and is genuinely offended and confused. How can Carline respond in a way that is respectful?

- Misha has been engaging in behavior that puts her well-being at risk. She has recently started drinking and using drugs, and she is rumored to be sleeping with more than one person. Her best friend wants to talk with her about respecting herself. What might she say to help Misha understand that she is worthy of respect?

- Josiah is frustrated that his principal is always on his case about the way he dresses. Josiah doesn't like to wear a belt, so his pants tend to sag, and he always forgets to take off his hat when he comes into the building. How might his principal approach Josiah in a way that is respectful so that Josiah will adhere to the school's dress code? How might Josiah respond in a way that is respectful to his principal? What would be the benefit of a respectful response?

- Dimitri and Trish have strong differing opinions in an immigration discussion taking place in a government class. How might each of them express their opinions in a way that is respectful? What advice would you give the teacher to ensure that the debate is respectful?

In addition to brainstorming with others, secondary students can role-play using these scenarios. I suggest a three-part role-play. One participant role-plays the first person in the scenario, the second participant plays the other person, and the third participant is the "observer." This person comments on the scene with observations and reflections. Then the students try the scene again, possibly switching roles.

At any grade level, the most important strategy for teaching respect is modeling respect and creating an environment in which respect is expected. When we are calm, considerate, and thoughtful in our responses to others, we demonstrate a way of being that is consistent with respectful behavior, regardless of the level of our understanding of another's cultures, customs, ways, or actions. This also includes our setting an expectation for respect regardless of our role at school. A school secretary, for example, is often the first person students and their parents encounter upon entering the school. If this is your role, your ability to greet and interact with them in a respectful way sets a tone for the entire school. A parent may come to the front office disgruntled and disrespectful. Your response can dictate if the situation is deescalated or aggravated and can be a model of appropriate behavior for any observer. Or, if you are a classroom teacher and you allow unruly behavior in your classroom, soon the students will believe that you do not care about respect. Their behavior as a whole will likely degenerate until you are in a position in which you feel your only hope to regain the class's attention is to resort to disrespectful behavior yourself, for example, by yelling at students or calling out a student in front of others. On the other hand, when students notice you acting respectfully and realize that you expect respectful behavior, they are more likely to act respectfully themselves and also expect respect from their peers. In the end, with respect as the standard for classroom behavior, the young people within our care at school will demonstrate an ability to interact with others socially in a way that is civil, considerate, and courteous, and they will be aware of the importance of doing so.

It Takes a Humble Person to Let Go of His or Her Own Perspective in Order to See Someone Else's

A quote by Henri-Frederic Amiel leads us into our next component of social awareness: the idea of cultural humility. Philosopher Amiel (2016) said, "There is no respect for others without humility in one's self." A key to being more socially aware is the ability to possess and practice humility. Humility is defined as "freedom from pride or arrogance" (*Merriam-Webster Dictionary*, 2018a). Humility, then, can help people have curious and open hearts when getting to know others. Research done in the realm of therapeutic practice suggests that humility can be crucial in developing bonding relationships, because individuals are inclined to value their own perspective (Davis et al., 2013). It takes a humble person to let go of his or her own perspective in order to see someone else's.

IMPLICIT BIAS JUSTIFIES
A NEED FOR CULTURAL HUMILITY

In the world of education, we tend to use the phrase *cultural competence* when referring to understanding, appreciating, and respecting another's culture so that we can build meaningful relationships with our colleagues, students, and families. If we are culturally *competent,* it is assumed that we understand everything there is to know about another's culture, when actually, we don't. Perhaps then, *cultural humility* is a more appropriate term. The Aspen Institute and educators across the nation recognize a need for cultural humility because, as addressed in Chapter 2, disproportionality does in fact exist in education. According to the Aspen Institute (2018), "U.S. schools systemically provide fewer resources to students of color and students from low-income families, including less funding, fewer enrichment activities, less rigorous coursework, lower-quality materials and other physical resources, curriculum that doesn't reject their background and culture, and unequal access to highly effective teachers" (p. 1). Furthermore:

> Most educators and school system leaders have good intentions and are committed to equity. But good intentions do not obviate the need to understand historical context and the role of race, racism, white privilege, and implicit bias in holding students back. Research indicates that teachers, like everyone, are subject to implicit biases associated with race and ethnicity, which can affect their judgments of student behavior and their relationships with students and families. (p. 3)

Acknowledgment of the potential for implicit bias justifies a need for cultural humility. In another body of work regarding therapeutic practice (Hook, Davis, Owen, Worthington, & Utsey, 2013), researchers find that

> Therapists who are culturally humble not only strive to be effective but also cultivate a growing awareness that they are inevitably limited in their knowledge and understanding of a client's cultural background, which motivates them to interpersonally attune themselves to the client in a quest to understand the individual client's cultural background and experience. (p. 354)

HUMILITY SEEKS TO UNDERSTAND

Educators who are culturally humble will do the same as the therapists mentioned above. Our clients are our students and their families. And their culture includes any beliefs, social norms, or traits that describe them based on race, ethnicity, gender, sexual orientation, language, disability, family background, family income, citizenship, or tribal status. Humility seeks to understand, so with a humble heart, we must show our students and their families through our words and actions that we want to know more about who they are, what they believe, and where they come from. It is our responsibility to learn the familial and cultural social norms practiced by the people who make up our school community.

As we think about practicing cultural humility, please consider a student you would like to understand better. Respond to the statements below in your quest to gain perspective. As you contemplate your responses, remember the idea from Chapter 1 about the questions we ask and *how* we ask the questions. "Tell me more . . ." is a powerful strategy that demonstrates cultural humility.

Practicing Cultural Humility

Write one acknowledgment of a specific issue, way of being, confusing behavior, or form of communication that you do not understand about the student:

- _____

Write two questions that you could sincerely ask the student to gain insight into his or her upbringing or home life?

- _____

- _____

In two different ways, write a question that might provide you with insight into who or what the student values:

- _____

- _____

In two different ways, write a question that might provide you with insight into the student's feeling about school:

- _____

- _____

How might you word a question to sincerely gain insight regarding the student's belief in his or her ability to achieve academically:

- _____

---

online resources | Available for download at **resources.corwin.com/StartWithTheHeart**

Cultural humility goes a long way in creating a space that is safe, nonjudgmental, and accepting. In such a space, we create an environment in which we help our students recognize the needs of other people. From joining someone we see sitting alone at lunch to noticing when someone is being teased on the bus and choosing to defend that person, our students have opportunities to show respect and humility by helping others within our school communities. If we want our students to look beyond themselves to the needs of others, then we must be sure they understand the concept of empathy and learn to practice it.

EMPATHY IS ASSOCIATED WITH AN AUTHENTIC QUEST FOR UNDERSTANDING

Empathy is another component of social awareness. Some students empathize with others naturally. They are able to put themselves in the shoes of another person and seek to understand what that person may be feeling or experiencing. But other students don't understand the concept of empathy, let alone practice it. People sometime confuse empathy for sympathy. Sympathy is generally associated with feeling pity or sorry for someone. But empathy is associated with an authentic quest for understanding what it might be like for a person as he or she experiences challenges or hardship, recalling the old adage of "walk a mile in my shoes." Whereas sympathy says, "I'm sorry for you," empathy says, "I am here for you." If sympathy expresses, "I feel bad for where you have been and what you have gone through," then empathy asserts, "I will travel with you."

USE ACADEMICS TO TEACH EMPATHY

We can use academics to teach empathy. Using stories from literature, lessons from history, or challenging math problems or science concepts, we can find the basis for discussing the relationships between an experience and the feelings that may result. Students can speak, listen, write, and engage in productive discourse based on examples of circumstances that require empathy or recognition of when empathy does or does not occur in a given situation. For example, *To Kill a Mockingbird* is required reading for many high school English classes and is full of characters who demonstrate empathy: from Atticus's defense of Tom, who unlike Atticus, is black and accused of rape, to Scout's support of Boo, the town recluse. Both Atticus and Scout must put themselves in the shoes of Tom and Boo in order to defend them, and they are only two of the many characters throughout the book who demonstrate empathy. Students can write about these characters and compare and contrast the various ways they empathize. *Wonder,* by R. J. Palacio, is a more contemporary book that provides a variety of scenarios about which discussions or writing assignments could be created to explore the significance of empathy and the life lessons that can be found within situations in which characters seek to understand and be there for one another.

As another example, a math class might find a teacher introducing the concept of empathy by asking students to engage in a brief discussion regarding how they feel when a math problem is difficult to understand. Students can each share what they notice regarding their thinking and the physical response in their bodies when they are frustrated or confused about a math problem. This will give those for whom math comes easy the opportunity to empathize with those who struggle and, in doing so, sets the tone for understanding and consideration in the classroom. The teacher may also guide the students in discussing how someone might feel and perform if he or she is confused and the entire class lacks empathy versus what might happen if they choose to empathize with the confused student.

Statistics can be used in any class, at any grade level, to create opportunities for productive and empathetic discussions. For example, the Human Rights Campaign (2017) surveyed 10,000 youth, ages 13–17, who identify as LBGTQ. They found that

> LGBT youth are more than two times as likely as non-LGBT youth to say they have been verbally harassed and called names at school. Among LGBT youth, half (51%) have been verbally harassed at school, compared to 25% among non-LGBT students. [Additionally,] LGBT youth are twice as likely as their peers to say they have been physically assaulted, kicked or shoved at school. Among LGBT youth, 17% report they have been physically attacked often while 10% of their peers say the same.

These statistics may seem to tread on sensitive waters, but it is imperative to address them through an empathetic lens, because the plight of students who identify as LGBTQ is based in a reality that can result in bullying, depression, and suicide. Useful questions to ask are, "Why do you think people who identify as LGBTQ are more likely to be verbally or physically harassed at school?" or "What could you do to demonstrate empathy for someone who identifies as LGBTQ?" Students could also discuss ways to help aggressors better understand the people they are harassing. *Welcoming Schools,* a project of the Human Rights Campaign Foundation (welcomingschools.org), provides resources and lesson plans for schools that promote inclusive, safe, and welcoming environments for all students and families with an emphasis on preventing bias-based bullying, inclusion of students who identify as LGBTQ and their families, and supporting diversity. Additional topics for which statistics could be used to prompt empathy lessons might include bullying, mental health, or equity in schools.

CLEAN UP THE GOOP

We can also help our students develop empathy by asking them how they believe an action or behavior on their part might affect how another person feels. For example, ask, "How might a new student be feeling upon entering the classroom if all the students ignore him?" When students understand that being kind and welcoming the new student to the classroom demonstrates empathy, it makes the abstract concept more easily understood. This is especially valuable in lower grade levels. As another example, when I lead student assemblies in elementary school, or speak in classrooms where the theme is about acceptance and kindness, I often call up a student volunteer. I then make a big show of squeezing all of the toothpaste out of a tube in front of me so that it falls on the floor in a big pile of goop. As the student looks at the toothpaste, I hand her the tube and ask, "Can you please put it back in the tube for me?" All the kids laugh when the student commonly replies, "No way! That would be impossible!" And I use that as a segue to explain that the toothpaste is an analogy for the hurtful and unkind things that we say and do to our peers. There are ways to make it right, or "clean up the goop," so to speak, as we will discuss in Chapter 6, but we can't take back our words and actions.

For older students, we can use commonalities to develop empathy. For example, human beings tend to judge people based on how they look or act without necessarily understanding what a person has been through. This is what happened in my sister Kelly's case. I suggest two incredibly powerful activities to teach empathy to older students: Aces and Faces, and Cross the Line. Both activities should be used with students in sixth grade or higher. They require an ability to role-play and assimilate feelings that may be difficult for younger students to process. Unless students have demonstrated maturity and can meet expectations for seriousness, sincerity, respect, and trustworthiness, these activities should *not* be used. Even if they're not there yet, these activities are worth learning about while you put in the time and effort that it may take to bring your students to this place of maturity.

ACES AND FACES

Aces and Faces (Figure 5.2 on the next page) is an activity that simulates what it might be like to be in a stereotypical group at school. It helps students to experience what it might feel like to be admired, tolerated, ignored, or bullied. Give each student a playing card and ask them not look at it. They are to hold the card against their chests while you explain the instructions. When you say so, the students are to turn their cards out-facing, without looking at what is on their own, and hold them against their foreheads. They are now able to see everyone else's. At your request, students are to mingle, and without indicating the number or face card that a person is showing, they are to "act" in a way that treats each person as delineated in the accompanying diagram.

As the instructor, allow the activity to go on for about three to four minutes. Within this time, you will see that the students with the higher cards tend to group together, while those with the lower cards may be found on the outside of the group, often standing alone. Once you stop the activity, you can ask the students

FIGURE 5.2

Aces and Faces

You will all be given a card. Do not look at it.
When I say, please turn the card away from
you and hold it up on your forehead. Then as you
encounter people, treat them as instructed:

Treat people accordingly:

- A–J: Treat these people with
  respect. Compliment them.
  Ask to hang out. You like them
  and want to be in their presence.
- 10–8: Accept these people.
  Be nice, but don't make much
  of an effort to include them.
- 7–5: Ignore these people.
  Show complete disregard.
- 4–2: Make fun of these
  people. Put them down.

IMAGE SOURCE: Pixabay.com/en/users/Clker-Free-Vector-Images-3736/

to look at their cards. Then pull students together to process what happened with questions such as the following:

- Without knowing what your card was, how did you feel? What did this feeling make you think your card was?

- Was your feeling unique for you? Why or why not?

- What did you notice about other people as this activity progressed?

- What was difficult or challenging about treating people as the instructions directed?

- How might the feelings you experienced in this activity be applied to everyday life at school?

- What other reflections do you have about this activity?

The processing portion of this activity cannot be neglected. Also, with some classes it may be advisable to strategically assign cards. A student who tends to be shy and often alone may "coincidentally" get an ace while a student who tends to tease others may get a 2. This particular strategy is helpful in creating the biggest impact on all students. I have always found the Aces and Faces activity awakens social awareness and empathy, even with adult groups.

CROSS THE LINE

Cross the Line is another activity that creates empathy in that it helps people realize they are not alone, and it causes epiphanies for students who may have assumed or made judgments about other human beings in the group. This activity, too, requires seriousness and maturity. In fact, if students are unable to follow instructions or maintain silence throughout the activity, then I do not recommend you use this activity. I also discourage this activity if a teacher has yet to establish a classroom management style that fosters respect and attention to task. One more important qualification: if the activity is being used during a schoolwide event, the administrator or activity leader must have command and control of the entire group and the ability to establish a sense of commitment and trust.

Cross the Line is fairly simple in format but intricate in expectations. Ask everyone to gather on one side of the room in a line and face toward its center. Place a piece of tape so that it is stretched out from one end of the room to the other, about ten feet in front of the line of people. Ask everyone to become silent to listen to the instructions. Also ask students who are close friends or in a relationship to make sure they are not standing next to each other in order to minimize distractions. Instructions should sound something like this:

First and foremost, this is a silent activity. It requires listening with your heart. Therefore, there is to be no talking, snickering, giggling, or any other nonverbal messages that might communicate judgment. Second, the activity requires dignity and respect for every person involved. This is how the activity works: I will call out specific categories/labels/descriptions in the form of a statement, and ask that all of those to whom this applies walk across the line and then turn and face those who did not cross. For example, I might request that anyone with glasses please cross the line. If this describes you, and you feel comfortable acknowledging it, you would walk just past the line of tape on the floor. Only you can determine if a statement is authentic or true to you. For example, I might cross the line because I wear contacts during the day but glasses at home. Although no one may know that I wear glasses, the statement is true to me. Once you've crossed the line, turn and face the crowd you just left. I will give you a few seconds to make observations of people on both sides of the line and to connect with your feelings. Then when I say, "You may return," silently return to the side you started from. After a few seconds, I will continue

(Continued)

with a new statement. Remember, there is no pressure to cross the line if you don't feel comfortable doing so. You will need to make that decision. The statements that are asked during this activity will go from low-risk statements to very personal, higher risk statements. At the conclusion of the activity, we will discuss what we felt and what we learned. There may be times when this activity makes you feel slightly uncomfortable. I would urge you to lean into that discomfort, since it may mean that you are about to gain an important learning or insight about yourself and others. Remember the goal throughout the activity is to make sincere and silent observations and to respond to each statement with your authentic truth.

Potential statements for Cross the Line range from low-risk questions such as: Please cross the line . . .

- If you have siblings who look up to you

- If you have ever been out of this country

- If you have experienced a time in your life that brought you joy

- If you consider yourself a confident person

- If your natural parents are divorced

. . . to higher risk questions such as: Please cross the line . . .

- If you have been hurt by someone you love

- If you have had an immediate family member pass away (mom, dad, brother, or sister)

- If you are in pain

- If you or someone in your family is gay, lesbian, bisexual, or transgender

- If you or someone in your immediate family has ever been homeless

- If you or an immediate family member has attempted suicide

- If you or someone in your immediate family has experienced drug addiction or alcoholism

I always end the activity with the following two statements: Please cross the line . . .

- If by doing this activity you realize you are not alone
- If you feel you have gained insight about at least one other person in this room by doing this activity

I suggest having a counselor present during this activity and discussing the importance of confidentiality, as well as mandated reporter responsibilities, before you begin because the processing may stimulate sharing that is emotional and personal. I also encourage the adults in the room to participate as well (with the exception of the person serving in the role of Instructor/Activity Leader). Following the activity, it is important to bring the group together for processing. Processing questions can be as simple as the following:

- What did you feel as we started this activity? How about during the activity? Did your feelings change throughout?
- What did you notice during this activity?
- How might this activity help you to see others differently?
- How might this activity help a person to have empathy?

This activity is powerful, but it must be done with conscientious expectations of respect in order for students to experience sincere compassion and value the opportunity for empathetic response. Also, in order to decrease the level of risk for this activity (specifically for younger adolescents or if trust has not been established previously), I recommend deleting "you" from any of the personal statements, and replacing it with "someone you know." This modification still elicits an empathetic response due to an increased awareness of who has been exposed to which difficult situations, but it takes away the individual identification of feeling or experience.

Please reflect on both activities with the question below that is most appropriate for your role:

1. If you work with younger students, how might you modify one of the activities so that it is age appropriate?

   _____

   _____

   _____

   _____

   _____

2. If you work on the playground or in the front office, the lunchroom, or the counseling office, how might participating in or observing one of these activities help you in your role with students?

_____

_____

_____

_____

_____

3. If you work with older students, how might you extend one of these activities with a future lesson?

_____

_____

_____

_____

_____

One of the expressions often shared during Cross the Line processing is, "I had no idea . . . [he had been homeless . . . that she didn't have confidence in herself . . . that he was struggling with addiction]." You can complete the sentence with any statement that was used for the activity. The point is that there are things we don't know or understand because we haven't experienced these things ourselves.

CREATE AN EXPECTATION FOR YOUR STUDENTS TO SERVE OTHERS

Serving within one's community also helps our students to develop empathy and become more socially aware of the challenges and hardships that others face. Again, I realize that time is not something at your disposal as an educator, so as much as creating a class community service project is ideal, you can also create an expectation for your students to serve others on their own or with their peers or family outside of school. The awareness, however, can be initiated in school. Social justice themes can be incorporated into any academic lesson. It seems most obvious in social studies to investigate social justice issues through past injustices or current events that jeopardize the health and welfare of human beings. But a lesson could be taught in math class by researching the cost of treatments for cancer and calculating out-of-pocket expenses based on a specific insurance coverage. Looking at the numbers may motivate students to act. Maybe they will see a fundraiser in the newspaper for someone who is living with cancer and want to contribute.

In fact, reading the newspaper is an ideal place to increase awareness of the various needs within a community. A small group "search and synthesize" activity allows students to work with peers to find a need in the community and then make a plan together to meet that need given predetermined resources. On a grander scale, if a philosophy of social, emotional, and academic development is being implemented school- or districtwide, I suggest adopting a policy wherein a community service project or a certain number of hours given in service to the community might substitute for one grade on an exam or one paper. Obviously, this type of policy requires prearranged and specific guidelines, but it encourages involvement and makes an impact on the community. Regardless of students' ages, ideas tend to flow and students become socially aware of the needs, challenges, and opportunities within the community.

Ultimately, having the ability to view situations from another's perspective, respecting oneself and others, approaching people with cultural humility, practicing empathy, and serving others are all ways in which to appreciate diversity and gain social awareness. Maya Angelou encouraged parents to "teach young people early on that in diversity there is beauty and there is strength" (Angelou, 2014). Within our various roles in the school system we can take up this task, too. Truly, it goes back to approaching all people and situations through a lens of love. We all have so much to learn from one another. No matter if a person is brown, black, yellow, white, red, or green, like my sister; no matter if living in poverty or with financial means; if male, female, a blend of both, or neither; no matter one's religion, relationship with their God, belief in science, or both, we are all human beings who have the ability to learn from, appreciate, honor, and love one another. Being socially aware can only help us to grow into responsible individuals who can build meaningful relationships with others.

In the boxes that follow, you'll hear from students sharing what they think you should know about social awareness and their suggestions for teaching the competency.

What You Should Know . . . Social Awareness

Straight From the Hearts of Students

- *I am observant. I notice a lot of things about people and their emotions. Especially when a student's feelings are hurt because of something that a kid or teacher says.*

- *I want you to know that not everybody is happy or has had a perfect life.*

- *I don't get along with certain kids.*

(Continued)

(Continued)

- *I hate when people come up and just push my wheelchair from behind without telling me they are there.*
- *I am very aware of life from other kids' perspectives. I may not have experienced what they experience, but I can easily put myself in their shoes and see all sides of the story.*
- *I can understand what others are feeling, but it is harder for me to be able to take their perspective.*
- *My family practices the Old Ways.*
- *I like to be alone. I get uncomfortable in social situations.*
- *Just cuz I'm brown doesn't mean I'm in a gang.*
- *The reason I don't do my homework is because we don't have electricity because we sleep in our car.*

- *Most of my teachers don't look like me. I think they don't understand me.*
- *I would like to learn about other kids' lives, but I don't know how to ask.*
- *Sometimes I can get very frustrated with others.*
- *Without my hearing aids, I can't hear the teacher.*
- *I don't want everyone to know that we can't pay our bills.*
- *I feel like my teachers judge me because I'm transgender. I'm still just a kid who wants to learn.*
- *I love the color of my skin and the traditions in my family.*

As you've done in previous exercises, please identify a student you know who might have expressed emotions similar to one of those expressed in the "What You Should Know" box. With the knowledge you have today or the insight gained from reading these messages, please describe a way you might have changed your interaction with this student or with an entire class in order to help him, her, or them to develop the competency of social awareness:

_____

_____

_____

_____

_____

Here are the suggestions from students to help us, as educators, to be more socially aware and to encourage us to help our students to be more aware in regard to others. As you review the suggestions, highlight two or three that resonate with you.

Suggestions From Students . . . Social Awareness

- Include everyone. Some teachers leave the same kids out of discussions every day. It's not fair.

- Treat everyone the same. This shows students how to be accepting and fair, too.

- I have a teacher who says he teaches students, not lessons. All teachers should think this way.

- Be an example for students by not judging or discriminating against students you don't understand or like.

- You should do ongoing activities on how to put yourself in another person's shoes.

- Teach about other cultures. Even in math or science or PE, we can learn from other cultures.

- Pay attention.

- All students should share their stories. This will evoke empathy.

- Teach kids how to recognize how someone else is feeling.

- You should make sure everyone in a class knows what the appropriate social responses are. I'm surprised that sometimes kids haven't been taught to say "please" or "thank you," or just to have good manners.

- School should have activities during all classes that give time for all students to interact with each other.

- I am uncomfortable in social situations. It would help if teachers did activities that make me feel comfortable working with other kids.

- Play that telephone game with small groups but tell all the groups the same thing. See what they come up with in the end. It is funny and might show how people hear the same thing but think differently about it.

- Use role-playing to help students understand someone else's situation.

- Explain things in the students' modern language. Don't be phony, but it helps me to learn when the teacher speaks my language.

(Continued)

- Give information about social skills.

- Try to understand where a student is coming from. If you don't, ask questions.

- Talk to students privately if they are rude or need to fix their behavior, because it is embarrassing when it happens in front of other kids.

Please list below some strategies that you might use to foster the highlighted suggestions or to correct current instructional practices that inhibit them. Don't forget to brainstorm potential strategies with a colleague if you have difficulty thinking of strategies on your own.

- *Student suggestion:*

  _____
  _____
  _____

  o *Potential strategy:*

  _____
  _____
  _____

- *Student suggestion:*

  _____
  _____
  _____

  o *Potential strategy:*

  _____
  _____
  _____

- *Student suggestion:*

  _____
  _____
  _____

- *Potential strategy:*

  _____

  _____

  _____

As we conclude this chapter, please share one behavior, action, or instructional tactic that you will start, one that you will stop, and one that you will continue in regard to social awareness:

Start, Stop, Continue . . . Social Awareness

I will START:
I will STOP:
I will CONTINUE:

online resources ☞ Available for download at **resources.corwin.com/StartWithTheHeart**

1. Look back through the chapter and highlight one interesting point or story that resonates with you and explain why it made an impact.

2. Compare the difference between the terms *cultural competence* and *cultural humility*. Which term appeals to you more and why?

3. Please describe a lesson you have taught or observed that uses academics to teach empathy.

4. How do you choose to model empathy?

5. Have you ever said something to a student or colleague that you wished you hadn't? How did you "clean up the goop?" In reflection, what advice would you give yourself today?

6. Have you been involved in community service at your school? If so, please describe an experience that stands out to you. If not, how might you create this type of opportunity at your school?

7. Please select three bulleted items from the "What You Should Know" box that you feel are most important. Explain your reasons for prioritizing these items.

8. The Aspen Institute released an article titled "Pursuing Social and Emotional Development Through a Racial Equity Lens: A Call to Action" in May 2018. Read the article, which can be found at https://www.aspeninstitute.org/publications/pursuing-social-and-emotional-development-through-a-racial-equity-lens-a-call-to-action/. What is one paragraph from the article that resonates with you, and why?

 Available for download at **resources.corwin.com/StartWithTheHeart**

CHAPTER 6

Relationship Skills

The Significance of Being Seen and Heard

I answered my phone and heard, "T?" and then silence. "I lost another one, T," and then sobbing. I realized it was Cisco on the other end, and my heart just broke. I didn't know why he was so upset or the specifics behind his loss, but I knew he was hurting and he chose to reach out. "Tell me . . ." was all I said. And in small bursts of emotion, Cisco was able to share that his second close friend had been killed. Just six months prior, his best friend, another former student of mine, was killed in a hit-and-run accident. It was still unsolved, although there was speculation of drugs, alcohol, or gang involvement. And now, another friend, one he considered a brother, was killed by gunshot. Cisco didn't know what to do or where to turn, and he called me. I was at a loss. I don't know that anyone knows what to *do* in such a situation, but most of us know how to *be*. I could be quiet, a listening ear; be calm, a comforting word; and be compassionate, an open heart. I could physically be there for Cisco and offer to help. I could encourage him to know it was okay to cry and that his journey through grief was not one he would travel alone. I could be there for Cisco, because I had built a trustworthy relationship with him.

In fact, it didn't start out that way. Initially Cisco was very wary of me, certain I was out to get him because I had busted him for using drugs. He thought I was especially hard on him, and I admit I was. In fact, my approach with all of my students was always through the lens of love, while maintaining a fine balance between encouragement and firm boundaries with high expectations. As his principal, I saw in him an intelligence that I didn't think he knew he possessed. I saw the way that he had compassion for others, even though he acted so tough on the outside. And I saw that, despite his gang mentality, he was an individual with creative talent and hope in the future. Eventually, Cisco began to understand that these things I saw in him were actually my belief in him, and he began to trust me, and believe in himself too. Fortunately, I was not the only person at school with whom Cisco built relationships. He developed and maintained relationships with specific staff members, teachers, and his peers. It is evident to me that all of these relationships contributed to Cisco's graduating after having a positive experience in school, leading to academic achievement and a hopeful future. We can never disregard the impact of relationships on our students. Cisco's graduation speech, in the form of a spoken word piece, says it best:

Let me start off by saying . . .

School wasn't for me

I didn't respond well to authority

And never treated it like a priority

So, I spent the majority of my teenage stage

Engulfed in rage

From a young age

I was labeled a troubled kid

For the mistakes I made

All the dumb things I did since the 2nd grade

I was brought up in Sacramento County

I thought I was mad tough

Fought anyone who talked too much about me

I've been suspended 20 something times

And expelled twice

Lord knows I've struggled and tried to walk the straight line

The Lord also knows I've stolen, lied and threw up gang signs

When I moved to Douglas

I guess I couldn't help but start a ruckus

Got expelled from middle school for carrying a substance

Got sent to ASPIRE, a blessing in disguise

Even though I didn't realize at the time

To my surprise, ASPIRE welcomed me in

The first day I arrived I was told we all deserve a 2nd chance

Something I've never received

It really opened up my eyes

Walking thru the building I didn't feel criticized

But I still doubted myself

I thought I was forever lost

Until Ms. Hipple's path crossed mine

She was the first teacher to lend me help

She wasn't going to let me fall behind

For the first time, I felt motivation

But ASPIRE did more than give me an education

It helped break down the walls I set

I never had teachers who wanted to have a conversation

They set me straight when my expectations weren't met

Because I have aspirations and they never let me forget

Thank you ASPIRE, I can't state it more simple

Thank you for introducing me to the incredible Ms. Hipple

Even the new Ms. Nicoll, who grew on me fast

Ima miss sitting in your class, sharing our past

One of the simple things that made me feel not so lonely

Ranting about TV shows and music with Ms. Rohde

Mr. Herald whose philosophies changed my way of thought

To Ms. Caralee, thank you for all the passion and love you brought

Mr. Nair, with crazy stories that added insight

And Mr. Emm . . . ehh, I guess you're alright (You know I love you Man)

Ms. Jen thank you for feeding me, we came a long way

Thank you, Renee for treating my headaches from day to day

T, thank you with everything I have, for opening the door of opportunity

On to the next chapter in my life

but you will all be part of my story

So, let me finish by saying . . .

School wasn't for me, but I still finished

I wasn't going to diminish

All those years that I pushed my limits

Just to quit . . . my mom brought me into this world, so Ima honor it,

And all her sacrifices,

As I stand here with my scholarship

"LEARNING REQUIRES POSITIVE RELATIONSHIPS"

Cisco's belief that the relationships he had with the adults in his life at school, and with his mom at home, led to his ability to achieve academically and to graduate. Research supports his thinking. The effect of relationships specifically related to achievement is highlighted by work done by author and researcher John Hattie. According to Hattie and coauthor Klaus Zierer (2018),

> Learning requires positive relationships—whether between learners and teachers, or between learners and their peers. Instruction is, therefore, essentially built on a relationship building, and the more safe and trusting these relationships are, the more the child will learn. These positive relationships are the precursors to learning—they form a resource to be spent when in challenging situations—as then students need to feel much trust to ask for help, to try again, and explore openly with their peers. (p. 129)

Cisco's need for support when he called me was extreme and personal. Occasionally this is the case with our students. More often, though, to be successful in school, and in life, our students need to develop relationships and have relational skills that, as Hattie and Zierer suggest, enable them to "ask for help, to try again, and to explore openly with their peers." The Collaborative for Academic, Social, and Emotional Learning (2018) takes it a bit further and defines necessary relational skills as

> [t]he ability to establish and maintain healthy and rewarding relationships with diverse individuals and groups. This includes communicating clearly, listening actively, cooperating, resisting inappropriate social pressure, negotiating conflict constructively and seeking and offering help when needed.

The Aspen Institute also recognizes the importance of a mindset that encourages belonging as a domain for social and emotional development. In this chapter, we explore these concepts in the context of building relationships with our students and helping them to develop relational skills, starting with the idea of building trust because it is the foundation of healthy relationships.

In a PBS interview, James Comer (2005), founder of the Comer School Development Program and a professor of child psychiatry at Yale University said,

> It takes time to build trust, it takes time to build good relationships. You are not going to find a curriculum or an instructional approach anywhere that overcomes the distrust and alienation and anger and so on that slows the relationships and the learning that's possible. There is no magic pill.

If trust has a positive impact on relationship building and learning, then it is worth discussion. Developing trust is a journey, but there are things we can do along the way to build trust with our students. I have found that combining the Brown-Skinner Model for Building Trust (Brown & Skinner, 2007) with high expectations and consistent boundaries is most successful (see Figure 6.1).

Brown and Skinner developed this model as a technique for working with students who are considered "at risk." It doesn't matter if a student acts out behaviorally, struggles academically, or earns good grades and is well behaved. These steps will help to build trust and, thus, relationships. These steps are meant to build upon

FIGURE 6.1

The Steps for Building Trust

1. Listen
2. Validate
3. Problem Solve   =   **Hope**
4. Positive Regard

one another, beginning with listening. When we listen to our students and then validate their feelings or experiences, whether we agree with them or not, we lay bricks on the road to promoting trust. If our students know we are willing to listen, actively, without needing to correct, provide guidance, or "fix" a situation for them, we validate their worth and confirm that their concerns, curiosities, and experiences have value. Next, when we help our students' problem solve on their own or with peers, rather than giving them the answers or telling them what they should do, we demonstrate our trust in their intelligence and efforts. Finally, as we have discussed in previous chapters, when we show positive regard for our students, we remind them that we are seeing something positive in them, so, perhaps like Cisco, they will begin to see something positive in themselves. By following these steps, trust will be built, even for the student with whom you seem to have the most difficulty building a relationship.

FIRM, CONSISTENT BOUNDARIES ARE IMPORTANT

I have found these steps are most effective when combined with high expectations and firm, consistent boundaries. I have always told my students that I have incredibly high expectations of them and that I would not lower them. For if I kept them high, they were sure to meet them. If I compromised and lowered them, they would meet those, too, so why not keep them high? Keeping expectations high helps students begin to trust that you believe they are capable of achieving behaviorally and academically. Finally, boundaries. Firm, consistent boundaries are important because they allow students to trust that they are safe, both emotionally and physically. Think about it. This is why they tend to push the boundaries. Our students want to be reassured that the boundaries will hold (and if you are a parent reading this, the same applies to your children). If we adjust them or move them without a substantial and thoughtful reason, our students will not feel safe because the boundaries are not secure. Eventually, even if they push back, when we keep our boundaries firm and consistent, our students feel safe, trust will grow, and relationships will develop.

Please take a moment to reflect:

- What is one element of trust building (see the graphic in the preceding section) that you already practice? What do you notice about the way that it affects your relationships with students?

_____

_____

_____

_____

- What is one element that resonated with you as something you would like to put into effect? Where will you start?

_____

_____

_____

_____

_____

STUDENTS BENEFIT FROM OUR USE OF BODY LANGUAGE

Each of the steps for trust building requires effective communication skills. For educators, the way we communicate can alienate our students and colleagues or draw them nearer to us. We must remember that communication starts with no words at all. Our body language speaks volumes and can express to a person if we are excited, sad, angry, disappointed, or embarrassed. Take a moment to visualize what each of these five emotions might look like without words, only body language. We can visualize emotions because our bodies talk. Young people can be incredibly sensitive to body language. Used appropriately, it helps us to redirect, discourage, or dissuade a student who is engaged in negative behavior, without having to say a word. This might allow a student to save face in front of a class, which ultimately can be a seed of growth for a trustworthy relationship. Body language can also be used to show approval and foster confidence. Eye contact, smiling, and open arms are types of nonverbal communication that encourage and reassure. Our students benefit from our use of body language in our efforts to build relationships with them, but it is also valuable for them to understand and practice reading and using body language as a skill to foster healthy relationships with others.

Asking younger students to match body positions with particular emotions is a fun way to familiarize elementary-age children with body language as a form of nonverbal communication. When establishing expectations at the beginning of the year, it can be instructional and entertaining to allow secondary students to play Emotion Charades, a game in which the students pretend to be the teacher by acting out each emotion and having the other students guess the emotion being demonstrated. By following this activity with a discussion about the value of understanding body language, we provide an opportunity to laugh and share together, which also builds community within the classroom.

Finally, an essential nonverbal communication skill is listening. We demonstrate care and interest when we listen attentively. Sometimes when one person is talking to another, the person who is "listening" to the speaker isn't really listening but instead is thinking about what he or she wants to say in response. This type of listener is quick to give advice or share a story of his or her own that relates to what the first speaker is saying. When this happens, the person who is sharing may feel misunderstood or may feel that what he or she has shared has little value. By contrast, an attentive listener will listen to tone and feelings, as well as the words being spoken, and will respond with statements such as "Tell me more about . . . ," "What did you feel when . . . ," or "How did that affect . . . ," giving the person speaking additional opportunities to share and be heard and understood. A person who is a quality listener understands that communication can build healthy relationships, especially if the person with whom we are communicating feels heard and, therefore, valued.

STUDENTS ARE VERY AWARE OF HOW WE SPEAK TO THEM AND THEIR PEERS

The way in which we communicate verbally makes a difference in our relationships as well. When our words are kind and thoughtful, they honor the person with whom we are speaking. Students are very aware of how we speak to them and their peers. In fact, when I work in schools on climate, I often facilitate focus groups with students. When I ask them for advice they would like to give their teachers or administrators, they repeatedly say, "Treat kids the same." When I question them further, they express that kids know how a teacher or an adult in the school feels about them by the way they talk to them, or *if* they talk to them. They suggest that adults will say things without thinking that make some of them feel bad or judged, and they sense when teachers favor others by the words they use. We discussed mindfulness in Chapter 4. If we are mindful, noticing our thoughts and feelings prior to speaking, our words are more likely to be intentional and considerate.

Teaching this relational skill to our students will have an impact on their lives and well-being. Teaching awareness of tone, volume, and word choice through modeling and classroom activities will provide students with an essential skill for navigating relationships in school and in life. Giving students an opportunity to explore voicing specific words or terms in different ways can be a fun way for them to cognitively and kinesthetically experience this lesson. For example, allow pairs of students to discuss and demonstrate using someone's name and the phrase "come here" to communicate a message. Provide three message options: (1) "You are in trouble," (2) "I want to show you something," and (3) "Everything will be okay." For example, a student might say, "Mary, come here" in many different ways, depending on the message he wants to communicate. Having one partner verbalize the message to another person in each of the three ways in front of the entire class will be the cause for much laughter and cohesiveness, fostering productive social interactions at school. Ultimately, practicing appropriate verbal communication will provide awareness and skills that will benefit students in college and the workplace.

Cooperation and Working Together Are Valid Skills for Students to Learn and Practice

According to the National Association of Colleges and Employers, the ability to communicate verbally with people inside and outside an organization is the third most sought-after skill by employers nationwide. The employability skill that earned the number-one spot is the ability to work in a team structure (Adams, 2014). Thus, cooperation and working together are valid skills for students to learn and practice during school because these skills can transfer as an asset in the workplace. Teaching the skill of cooperation is a task that many kindergarten teachers have mastered. I have observed effective teachers facilitate opportunities for five- and six-year-olds to take turns or share in a way that empowers the students to cooperate with kindness and respect. Games that encourage students to work together can be fun for elementary and secondary students alike.

For younger students, an activity as fundamental as working together to keep a balloon in the air can foster cooperation but also provide a way to practice counting and adding. For example, create small groups (three or four students is the ideal) and give each group a balloon. Tell them that the goal is to keep the balloon in the air by taking turns touching it without letting it touch the ground. Students should be instructed to count out loud and record the highest number that is reached prior to the balloon touching the ground. If this activity is repeated, students can add their total number of touches. Older elementary students might find it challenging to create word problems including the number of touches and number of students in the group.

Team Work Is an Essential Life Skill

Secondary students can practice cooperation by working together on group projects in any subject. Giving roles to each individual ensures that all participants must cooperate in order to complete the project. Outside of academic classes, some schools allow time during homeroom or advisory to teach and practice social and emotional learning skills. Many activities promoting teamwork and cooperation can be facilitated during such a time. An activity I use to engage students, as well as adults, is the Knotted Shoelace.

This activity requires a shoelace for every participant. Prior to the activity, I tie three or four knots in each shoelace (depending on the participant's age, I vary the tightness of the knots). I ask each participant to hold one end of the shoelace between the thumb and forefinger of one hand. They are not allowed to let go of the shoelace for the duration of the activity. They are then asked, at my direction, to untie the knots using their other hand only. Participants often start out enthusiastic and confident but quickly realize the activity is challenging. I let the activity go on just long enough for most participants to express frustration or discouragement. At that point, I ask them to partner up with one or two other people and attempt the activity again, allowing them to use their free hands to work together on each other's shoelace. After the activity is completed, I ask the following questions:

- What feelings or thoughts did you notice when you attempted that activity on your own?

- Did those feelings or thoughts differ when you worked with another person?

- How did you solve the problem together, and how does that differ from your effort alone?

- What did you learn from this activity?

- Can you apply what you learned from this activity to school or to life outside of school?

The Knotted Shoelace is one activity of many. Many websites provide ideas and activities for teaching cooperation or teamwork. To find these, use your search engine and enter "teamwork activities for students." Many sites incorporate critical thinking, communication, or content-specific applications. Cooperative games or teamwork activities also provide students with an opportunity to collaborate and problem solve strategically. Ultimately, students learn that working productively with others contributes to goal achievement. Teamwork is a life skill that fosters patience, perseverance, and appreciation for individual strengths within a group. These skills are indispensable for strong social interactions, and they also support academic achievement.

LEARNING AND PRACTICING EFFECTIVE CONFLICT RESOLUTION SKILLS FOR STUDENTS AND SCHOOL EMPLOYEES MAXIMIZES LEARNING

In efforts to provide safe, respectful, and engaging environments for all, most schools institute processes to improve communication and resolve conflict. Conflict resolution is another vital component of the relationship skills competency. Conflicts in schools can create chaos and distract from learning. Therefore, learning and practicing effective conflict resolution skills for students and school employees maximizes learning, builds life skills such as problem solving, and grows healthy relationships. Mediation and restorative practices in response to conflict or situations that typically might call for disciplinary procedures are effective and constructive, rather than punitive. If you are reading this and thinking that a disregard for punitive discipline only reinforces negative behavior, then I challenge you to put into practice for at least three weeks one of the ideas described in the next two sections. I believe you will find students to be receptive, engaged, and more likely to change behavior. As an administrator, I was considered a firm disciplinarian, but not because my immediate response was punitive. Rather, I had high expectations for conflict resolution through accountability, problem solving, and sincere forgiveness.

CONFLICT MEDIATION

Conflict mediation is effective when conflict exists between two people or two groups of people. This process allows for an impartial mediator to serve as a facilitator, laying out ground rules that create conditions for success and constructive conversation. Conflict mediation can take place in the counselor's or principal's office, in the classroom, or on the playground. It is most successful when adopted schoolwide, with all personnel trained in facilitation. Peers can also serve as facilitators, but they too must be trained, and supervised by a qualified adult. Conflict mediation begins with both parties agreeing to participate in the mediation process and accepting a predetermined best alternative in case one or both parties resist or refuse mediation, or neglect to follow through with the resolution. The alternative to conflict mediation tends to be punitive rather that restorative, which encourages authentic effort in the process. A successful mediation includes attentive listening and respectful speaking. Both parties have an opportunity to share their views of the situation and are encouraged to share feelings and impact. Productive mediation involves cooperative problem-solving, including a plan to make amends and change behavior. The What Works Clearinghouse website (https://ies.ed.gov/ncee/wwc/), as well as other websites listed in Chapter 8, provide a variety of evidence-based behavioral interventions that incorporate conflict mediation.

RESTORATIVE PRACTICES

Restorative practices can include conflict mediation and a focus on repairing hurt or harm to another human being, group, or entity. A restorative practice approach tends to emphasize learning from an experience and making a sincere effort to make amends and value people. Restorative practices can be proactive in nature by establishing processes that create a family atmosphere within the school or classroom built on acceptance, respect, and trust. For example, a student, let's call him Greg, may be asked to account for his disrespectful behavior at recess. In this school, norms have already been established for a productive discussion in which anyone in the circle can share a concern for accountability. It can be the offender or anyone else in the group who has heard about or is aware of Greg's negative behavior. When Greg is called on his behavior, it is expected that he will explain the situation from his point of view, hopefully owning his wrongdoing. Through circle discussion led by a peer, teacher, or counselor, a plan might be made for Greg to make the situation right. He might be asked to identify individuals to whom he owes a sincere apology. The circle group, with Greg's input, might also determine appropriate amends or consequences. Finally, the circle might brainstorm ways in which Greg can act differently in the future to avoid disrespectful behavior. According to a practical and informative book appropriately titled *Better Than Carrots or Sticks: Restorative Practices for Positive Classroom Management* (Smith, Fisher, & Frey, 2017), "Restorative practices are predicated on the positive relationships that students and adults have with one another. Simply said, it's harder for students to act defiantly or disrespectfully towards adults who clearly care about them and their future" (p. 64). This book is a valuable resource, as it breaks down procedures and expectations, provides peace-building and peacemaking activities, and contains a chapter on creating a mindset for restorative practices. Another valuable resource is the International Institute for Restorative Practices website at https://www.iirp.edu/projects/safer-saner-schools.

Considering what you have just read, in addition to any practical experience you have had with conflict resolution, what is at least one benefit for each of the following categories:

1. *Students:*

   _____

   _____

2. *Teacher/leader:*

   _____

   _____

3. *Learning:*

   _____

   _____

4. *Classroom or school climate:*

   _____

   _____

Teaching Refusal Skills

Constructive resolution of conflict generally evolves from a situation in which relationships are built on trust and respect. These types of relationships allow for us to communicate clearly, even if we are uncomfortable in a social situation. Our students are never too young to learn the value of politely standing up for one's beliefs or desires, regardless of the behaviors from the majority of the group. We often hear the term *peer pressure* in the world of education. When I was a ninth-grade health teacher discussing alcohol and drug use with my students, they would often say, "Mrs. T, there is no such thing as peer pressure. We do what we do because we are curious." My follow-up question was always, "But, *why* are you curious?" Ultimately, through an engaging class discussion, students agreed they were not curious because they were watching their parents "have fun" drinking or getting high. (In fact, if drug or alcohol use was a part of their family culture, it was often a negative experience.) Their curiosity, rather, stemmed from watching their friends engage in drinking or using drugs, which led to a discussion about the idea of indirect peer pressure. Social pressure does not need to be "in your face" direct pressure. Students often *feel* pressure because the majority of other people around them are engaging and they don't want to be left out.

We can help our students resist negative social pressure by teaching them to use refusal skills with sincerity and assertiveness. I taught my students a five-step process:

1. *Use the word* **no.** Young people often say "I don't know" or "I don't think so" when being asked to take part in a behavior that makes them uncomfortable. It is imperative that they use the actual word *no* because it leaves no room for misunderstanding or confusion.

2. *Make eye contact.* Eye contact throughout the entire refusal process demonstrates assertiveness and sincerity.

3. *Give a long-term, personal reason with your refusal.* I learned as a ninth-grade teacher that many of my students were taught in elementary school to "just say no to drugs" by providing a temporary excuse, such as "I can't today, I have to babysit." I reminded my students that this type of response indirectly communicates, "So, ask me tomorrow. I might say yes." A long-term, personal reason such as "No, I choose not to use because I have an opportunity to be the first in my family to go to college and I don't want to do anything to jeopardize that" leaves no room for doubt about the seriousness of one's refusal.

4. *Suggest a positive alternative.* Suggesting an alternative activity is especially important if the relationship between the person or people who are providing the pressure and the one who is refusing is valued. An alternative allows the opportunity for the "pressurer" to save face and redirect.

5. *Walk away.* If a person has practiced steps one through four and the pressure continues, it is appropriate and necessary at that point to walk away. I would tell my students that at this point if a friend is not respecting your refusal, then he or she is not truly a friend.

After introducing the refusal skill process, it is beneficial to give students an opportunity to role-play in order to practice. I will never forget a young lady who came back to school after a weekend, and said, "Mrs. T, I thought it was so corny when you made us practice saying 'no' on Friday, but I was in a situation this weekend, and it actually worked!" Had this student not had the opportunity to practice, she may not have known what to say or do to get out of a socially uncomfortable or pressured situation. Elementary teachers can scale the steps down to provide students with skills to stand up for themselves on the playground or during class group work. If you work with young people at the secondary level, you might teach the skills one-on-one if appropriate when a student comes to you with a dilemma.

Consider your role within the educational system. When might you teach these skills to a student or group of students, and what might it look like?

Reflection on Teaching Refusal Skills

_____

_____

_____

_____

_____

_____

_____

_____

THE RELATIONSHIPS WE HAVE WITH OUR STUDENTS DETERMINE THEIR COMFORT LEVEL IN ASKING FOR HELP OR SUPPORT

Seeking or offering help are additional components of relationship skills. Many of us hesitate to ask for help. We are sometimes embarrassed to demonstrate vulnerability and express a need. Our students are much the same. However, when a relationship has been developed based on trust and open communication, it is easier to recognize needs or ask for support. It is important to admit that it is okay to seek help. Whether it is an extreme situation like Cisco's, in which he was reeling from a tragedy, or an academic circumstance in which a student doesn't understand a concept and is confused, the relationships we have with our students determine their comfort level in asking for help or support. Consider the students at your school who sit quietly in classrooms and don't participate in the class lesson. Is it that they truly do not want to be involved, or are they afraid to "look dumb" or reveal their confusion? If the class environment is one in which relationships have been built and expectations for an encouragement of curiosity and understanding have been set, then students tend to feel secure and able to ask for clarification or assistance from their teacher or peers. Remember that Hattie and Zierer (2018) said, "Learning requires positive relationships." University of Virginia professors Sara Rimm-Kaufman and Lia Sandilos (2018) concur and go on to justify the correlation between positive relationships and achievement:

> Improving students' relationships with teachers has important, positive and long-lasting implications for both students' academic and social development. . . . Those students who have close, positive and supportive relationships with their teachers will attain higher levels of achievement than those students with more conflict in their relationships. (para. 1)

In the end, students who have a positive experience seeking help are often the first to offer assistance when they see a need, both in class situations and in life. I remember taking Cisco to visit the mother of one of his friends who was killed. I sat and watched in awe as he took time to be there for her, to listen, and to do chores around her house. To this day, Cisco makes a point of being available for this grieving mother when a need arises. Their relationship began with her being the mother of his friend, and evolved into a person-to-person connection based on love and support.

A Relationship Built in School Can Be Lifelong

Finally, remember that the competency of relationship skills really revolves around love and connection. Refer back to the 7 Keys to Connection in Chapter 2 as you emphasize looking students and colleagues in the eye, using their names, and demonstrating your belief in them.

An enduring example of how a relationship built in a school setting can be lifelong is that of Kareem Abdul-Jabbar and his teacher, mentor, and coach, John Wooden. The accompanying photos demonstrate the power of that relationship. Coach

Wooden was known to say, "Seek opportunities to show you care. The smallest gestures often make the biggest difference" (Middleton, 2016). Wooden built relationships with his players, and others, by doing just that. The photo of Abdul-Jabbar holding Wooden's hand epitomizes the return on his sincere social investment.

■ *Left:* The Wizard of Westwood, Kareem Abdul-Jabbar, with Coach John Wooden at UCLA. *Right:* Abdul-Jabbar giving Coach Wooden a hand leaving the court after an NCAA anniversary celebration in 2007.

Sources: (left) AP Photo/stf *(right)* AP Photo/Gus Ruelas

Abdul-Jabbar (2017) said, "Coach Wooden and I shared our lives for more than four decades" (p. 227). *Shared lives:* what a phenomenal definition of relationship! Coach Wooden shared lives with his players because he set out to develop human beings, not athletes. In fact, he developed the Pyramid of Success based on character traits that he deemed necessary for success on the court and in life. Yet, at 98 years old, during a luncheon in his honor attended by many former players, including Kareem Abdul-Jabbar, Coach Wooden reflected on an essential trait that he had neglected to include in his pyramid. According to Abdul-Jabbar (2017), when Coach Wooden accepted his award, he looked out at all the people with whom he had shared his life and humbly told them, "Guys . . . I made a mistake, I left out love. And love is the most powerful word in our language and our culture" (p. 263). Coach Wooden may have left the word out of his Pyramid of Success, but he *lived* love and in doing so he developed relationships that lasted a lifetime and made an indelible impact on others. As educators, we too can love in this way as we connect with the people at school with whom we share our lives.

In the boxes that follow, you'll hear from students sharing what they think you should know about relationship skills and their suggestions for teaching the competency.

What You Should Know . . . Relationship Skills

Straight From the Hearts of Students

- *I am not trusting, so it is hard for me to talk to people I don't know.*

- *When you notice me get quiet, or lacking in my grades or sports, then something is wrong.*

- *I am a nice person, and I get along with others well. I don't understand when someone doesn't want to be around someone else.*

- *I can balance my relationships without much stress.*

- *I have good relationships because I try to never start rumors or drama.*

- *I'm good at handling my emotions in relationships, but I know a lot of people who aren't.*

- *I have very few relationships. I don't think there is any help for that, but I'd like to have more.*

- *I wish there was a class on how to make friends.*

- *I get judged for the people I hang out with. I think they are good people, and just*

- *because they make bad choices sometimes doesn't mean that's what I do.*

- *If you try to understand me, I think we will have a good relationship.*

- *I need help talking to other students in class because I have social anxiety.*

- *I think it is important that teachers maintain relationships with their students because then their students will want to come to class and learn.*

- *I sometimes think I upset someone, but then I find out that something or someone else did.*

- *I know I can be immature, and I am working on it.*

- *I want to have better relationships with people at school.*

- *I talk a lot. I know sometimes it bugs people. I have to learn how to listen.*

- *When I am in a relationship with a guy, sometimes I focus more on that than my school work.*

- *I need my teachers to be available for me to talk to them.*

- *Apparently, I have bad relationship skills even though I have many good friends.*

- *I don't know how to handle things if a relationship with a friend or girlfriend goes bad.*

- *My own relationship skills are average, although I am not that good at communicating clearly to express my needs.*

- *To have a good relationship with people at school, I think that we just need to be respectful of one another and treat others the way we want to be treated.*

- *I have one teacher that I connect with and he supports me. This makes a big difference for me at school.*

- *I have decent friendships but am too anxious to get involved in deeper relationships.*

- *When it comes to relationships, I keep disappointing myself and others so I stopped trying.*

As you've done in previous exercises, please identify a student you know who might have expressed emotions similar to one of those expressed in the "What You Should Know" box. With the knowledge you have today or the insight gained from reading these messages, please describe a way you might have changed your interaction with this student or with an entire class in order to help him, her, or them to develop the competency of relationship skills:

_____

_____

_____

_____

_____

Here are the suggestions from students to help educators build relationships with students and teach relational skills. As you review the suggestions, highlight two or three that resonate with you.

Suggestions From Students . . . Relationship Skills

- Put students in diverse groups for class projects. It helps them to get to know people they don't typically hang out with.

- If students are in a conflict with one another, sit them down and let them talk it out. Teach them how to solve conflicts in a positive way.

- Teach students how they might approach someone who is new.

- When someone has a problem, teach students how to help that person without solving the problem for them.

- Help students to understand how relationship skills are life skills.

- Hold an assembly that helps students build relationships with each other.

- Make sure there are a lot of clubs at school so that anyone can get involved and make friends.

- There should be an advisory class at every school to actually have time to build relationships with a small group of people. My school has 1,400 students, but we all have a chance to be close to everyone in our advisory class.

- It makes me uncomfortable when I see a lot of PDA. If you are the principal, you should make sure there is not too much in school.

- Have activities at lunch so students can get to know each other and so no one has to be alone if they don't want to.

- There should be support groups at school for people who are having a hard time with their parents or in other relationships.

- Teachers could create activities where students take turns working with random people so that people who don't have many friends get a chance to talk with other people.

- If you know that one of your students is in a bad relationship, say something and teach that person how to build a better one.

- Teach students how to identify abusive relationships and how to get out of them.

- Not every student has good relationship skills, so when they have to choose a group or a partner in class it can be awkward or uncomfortable. A teacher should find ways to group or partner students so that this doesn't happen.

- Teach students how to communicate, especially how to listen.

- Encourage students to meet new people or make new friends.

- Make sure students are nice to each other. This is probably the most important relationship skill.

- Provide activities that include socializing.

- If teachers want to build relationships with their students, they need to talk in a calm way, even if they are upset with a student.

- Teach students how to seek help.

- Teach students skills to communicate clearly, but help them put it in their own words.

- Kids might act like they hate it, but trust exercises help. Or games like the "name game" get kids to know each other's names, sparking curiosity and getting people to know others.

Please list below some strategies that you might use to foster the highlighted suggestions or to correct current instructional practices that inhibit them. Don't forget to brainstorm potential strategies with a colleague if you have difficulty thinking of strategies on your own.

- *Student suggestion:*

  _____

  _____

  _____

  o *Potential strategy:*

    _____

    _____

    _____

- *Student suggestion:*

  _____

  _____

  _____

  o *Potential strategy:*

    _____

    _____

    _____

- *Student suggestion:*

  _____

  _____

  _____

○ *Potential strategy:*

_____

_____

_____

As we conclude this chapter, please share one behavior, action, or instructional tactic that you will start, one that you will stop, and one that you will continue in regard to relationship skills:

Start, Stop, Continue . . . Relationship Skills

I will START:

I will STOP:

I will CONTINUE:

online resources ⟋ Available for download at **resources.corwin.com/StartWithTheHeart**

1. Consider Cisco's spoken word piece. Please circle words he uses that would have a positive effect on relationships and cross out words that may hinder positive connections. Choose one word from each category and explain your reasoning.

2. Reread CASEL's definition of relationship skills. Which behavior within the definition resonates with you as most important, and why?

3. How do listening actively, communicating clearly, and cooperating enrich the learning environment?

4. How much time do you spend within your school day actively engaging in building relationships and trust? What is the return on your investment?

5. How do you use body language to communicate in the classroom? Please think about a situation in which your body language or that of a colleague communicated in a way that made a student feel demeaned or embarrassed. Now reflect on a time that it was used to redirect a student in a positive way. Which is more beneficial, and why?

6. Realizing that fair is not equal, how do you demonstrate fairness? How do you model fairness so that *all* students can trust that you will be fair?

7. What might be the benefits of a restorative discussion between two staff members who are engaged in a conflict? Is there an opportunity within your school for this to take place? If not, how might you create such an opportunity?

8. Reflect on a relationship that began when you were a student that has continued today. Or, reflect on a relationship that you developed as an educator, with a student, that continues today. Why is that relationship important to you?

9. Consider the "Suggestions from Students" for this chapter. What additions might your current students contribute to this list?

 Available for download at **resources.corwin.com/StartWithTheHeart**

CHAPTER 7

Responsible Decision Making

The Power of Choice

Julius approached me with tears in his eyes as these words spilled from his lips: "Mrs. T, I don't know what to do. I think my girlfriend is pregnant." This is just one of the many encounters I have had with students over the years after they realized a decision they made might have detrimental or lifelong consequences. You have probably experienced similar conversations. If you are an educator of younger students, perhaps their dilemmas may not have life-changing consequences, but certainly you have dealt with a student who feels sad, confused, or angry in the aftermath of a choice he or she made that did not turn out as expected or desired.

Responsible decision making is the final competency we will discuss as a social and emotional learning skill. The Collaborative for Academic, Social, and Emotional Learning (2018) defines responsible decision making as

> the ability to make constructive choices about personal behavior and social interactions based on ethical standards, safety concerns, and social norms. The realistic evaluation of consequences of various actions, and a consideration of the wellbeing of oneself and others.

Ultimately, all of the competencies we have discussed thus far—self-awareness, self-management, social awareness, and relationship skills—contribute to our students' ability to make responsible decisions. Yet a few points of focus require further exploration: the power of choice, the process of decision making, the value of accountability, and finally, our instructional style.

As we consider the components of decision making and begin to guide our students through the process of developing good decision-making skills, it is helpful to note the biological aspects of our students' brains. According to current scientific research, most areas of the brain are undergoing major changes in our students (Jensen, 2005). Particularly in adolescence, brain cells are thickening and the area of the brain that controls executive functioning and is responsible for thoughtful decision making is "under construction." As a result, adolescent students may be impulsive, inattentive, and forgetful. The teen brain tends to lack forethought, so when we ask a teenager who made a poor choice, "Why did you do that?" and they respond, "I don't know," there may be underlying truth in their answer. This is why it is crucial for us to help our students develop skills that encourage cognizant thought and opportunities to practice making decisions. In his book *Teaching With the Brain in Mind*, Eric Jensen (2005) suggests that we be succinct; use modeling; help guide our students through decision making with discussion, not lecture; and be understanding rather than judgmental.

UNDERSTAND THE POWER BEHIND THE WORD CHOICE

In teaching, while supporting and applying responsible decision making in our schools, it is important that we help students acknowledge and understand the power behind the word *choice*. As we discussed in Chapter 4, too often students focus on external forces they feel to be responsible for negative experiences in their lives or for consequences they must face due to poor behavior. Our students can begin to work from their internal locus of control when they acknowledge that the choices they make have a direct effect on positive or negative outcomes. The first step is to guide students to begin using the word *choice*. When students make a poor choice, they tend to use the word *mistake*. Although the *Merriam-Webster Dictionary* (2018b) definition of *mistake* as "a wrong action or statement proceeding from faulty judgment, inadequate knowledge, or inattention" can easily be applied to a poor choice, it is critical to distinguish between these two terms. Students often brush off a poor choice as a mistake, without identifying what the *mistake* is and how they might correct it. In doing so, it allows them to use the word *mistake* as an excuse not requiring ownership. A *choice*, by contrast, has a connotation of control and empowerment. That is to say, we can choose differently; we can choose responsibly.

We are in the ideal position, as adults who work in a school setting, to teach our students the importance of making responsible choices. The choices our kids make can have consequential effects on their lives and the lives of others. Although young people may think about how a choice affects them, too often they fail to contemplate how it might affect others. Integrating lessons and providing applicable experiences and tools for students to learn about and practice responsible decision making, as well as how their choices impact others, is an important undertaking for educators. Opportunities arise every day in our schools and classrooms that allow our students to develop their decision-making skills so that they can transfer this ability to more complex or potentially life-changing decisions.

STUDENTS' ABILITIES TO MAKE RESPONSIBLE DECISIONS ARE INFLUENCED BY THEIR EXPERIENCES OUTSIDE OF SCHOOL

As we contemplate strategies for teaching decision-making skills, we must remember that although our students' abilities to make responsible decisions are influenced by their experiences at school, they are also influenced by their experiences at home and outside of school. I will always remember a young man enrolled in my school who, at 16 years old, did not demonstrate the basic manners that most have learned in our culture. At first, I thought maybe he was intentionally being disrespectful but soon learned that he hadn't been regularly exposed to typical social norms such as saying "please" and "thank you" or not cutting in line. I remember observing him in the cafeteria on his first day at our school. He pushed himself to the front of the line and said, "Give me pizza." The lunch lady responded with an incredulous, "Excuse me?" But this young man was completely unaware. His decisions about how he treated others had a great deal to do with how he had been allowed to behave at home or in public. His rude social behavior wasn't intentional in his eyes. He simply had not been exposed to the responsible choice associated with waiting patiently for his turn or communicating with common courtesy.

Likewise, an amazing teacher and extraordinary human being, Alecia Rohde, noticed recently that several of her high school students didn't seem to possess the social skills many of us take for granted. One girl in particular, Mrs. Rohde says, "Hawked loogies like a champ and had no idea it was socially unacceptable. She also had no filter and was rude on a regular basis. Through subtle social suggestions and modeling, she began to act more politely and, with that, her confidence began to grow." In addition to working one on one with this student, Mrs. Rohde also established a Healthy Choices group for interested young women to attend at lunch. This type of group would benefit any student interested in making responsible and appropriate choices. According to Mrs. Rohde,

We cover everything from basic hygiene to the complex nuances of teen relationships, to the manners needed when dining out. We also discuss safety issues like sex trafficking and setting boundaries. I choose some of the topics, but many of them are suggested by members of the group. I try to present discussion topics by separating the person from the behavior and I encourage the girls to know that their past actions don't define them. I tell them, "You can't start a new chapter in your life if you don't stop reading the last one." Now, our young women are finding their voices and developing a sense of self-confidence they didn't seem to have before.

WEAVE RESPONSIBLE DECISION MAKING INTO THE FABRIC OF OUR SCHOOLS

Mrs. Rohde created an extracurricular opportunity to incorporate the life skills required to address a specific need for a particular group of students. Yet there are general skills that can be presented to *all* students. For example, to weave responsible decision making into the fabric of our schools and classrooms, it is essential to introduce a decision-making practice or procedure. The following classic decision-making process has been reproduced in various forms over the years and gives us an operational basis for consideration when we teach decision making. Key steps include the following:

1. Identify the situation that requires a decision (realize that a decision needs to be made).

2. Gather relevant information:
   - Consider internal information based on core values and personal experience.
   - Consider external information such as pertinent research, expert analysis and evidence, and anecdotal experience.

3. Identify alternatives (based on the information gathered, there are likely several paths or options for action).

4. Weigh the evidence:
   - Consider the information gathered and how it fits into each alternative based on personal values, social norms, and general ethical standards.
   - Notice which alternative is supported by the most evidence.

5. Choose among the alternatives (determine which alternative is most likely to lead to a positive outcome).

6. Take action (choose—make the decision).

7. Review decision and its consequences as a result of the decision made:
   - Evaluate the results of the decision.
   - If the results did not lead to a positive outcome, consider modifications that would lead to a better situation in the future.

A similar process, based on the acronym DECIDE, tends to be more functional for teenagers because it is easier to remember and can easily be applied to a specific problem or concern (see Figure 7.1).

FIGURE 7.1

Define the problem

Explore the alternatives

Consider the consequences

Identify your values

Decide and act

Evaluate the results

In a student's mind, it may look like this:

D: *A new friend wants me to ditch class with her.*

E: *I could ditch class, I could ditch the beginning and show up late, or I could tell her no.*

C: *If I go to class, there are no negative consequences and I am present to learn the material. I won't fall behind. If I ditch, even for a short time, I miss the lesson and have to do make up work. I could also get in trouble at school and at home if I'm caught.*

I: *I have always been honest. I care about my grades and was taught to value my education. Relationships are also important to me. I have a good relationship with my teacher, and I'd like to have a better relationship with this friend.*

D: *I choose not to ditch. I am also going to let her know why and ask if she wants to hang out after school.*

E: *It was a responsible decision. The lesson in class was one I wouldn't have wanted to miss. My new friend acted frustrated with me at first, but we've been hanging out this week, and I think she understands that school is important to me.*

PROVIDE STUDENTS WITH AN OPPORTUNITY TO PRACTICE

Ideally, as with the use of refusal skills discussed in Chapter 6, we will find optimal success when we provide students with an opportunity to practice this process by thinking about a choice that needs to be made in the future and going through the steps mentally. For example, age-appropriate scenarios could be created as a role-play or discussion activity. Then, when the time comes to take action, the students have already determined the actions they are going to take. For teens, acting out scenarios—such as deciding whether to cheat on a test, to engage in sexual activity, or to sneak out of the house to go to a party—provides opportunities for them to mentally go through the decision-making process ahead of time, so that when the moment arises and a decision must be made, they will be more apt to make a responsible decision, because they have already thought through the decision and evaluated consequences and potential outcomes.

Younger students would benefit from applying a decision-making process as well. However, I advise scaling back the questions and putting them in age-appropriate language. It is helpful for younger students if the choices they need to make are fewer. Given two or three options, preselected by the teacher, students can practice decision making with support and structure. Consider the following examples:

- *You must read a book about transportation; here are three books to choose from.*

- *You may write your reflections in a journal or share verbally with your reading partner.*

- *You may finish your assignment during recess or take it home to finish tonight.*

Regardless of students' ages, learning and practicing decision making can be essential to helping them solve problems. Although the terms *decision making* and *problem solving* are often used interchangeably, they are not necessarily the same. One can make a decision absent a particular problem, such as deciding where to go for lunch. Or one can solve a problem without actually making a decision, such as when two students work together to determine the best way to build a tall tower. At the same time, overlap often exists between decision making and problem solving, and decision-making processes like DECIDE can certainly be modified, adapted, or used in their current form to assist students in solving problems.

Please consider your role as an educator and the way in which you have guided students in making decisions. Reflect on how you might use one of the ideas or processes described here to help your students gain decision-making skills. If you already teach a decision-making process, reflect on one idea from the reading that might enhance your instruction:

_____

_____

_____

_____

_____

_____

_____

_____

_____

Check Out the Hand

When our students engage in a decision-making process, they often make thoughtful and responsible decisions. However, in reality students are going to make irresponsible choices occasionally. It is also human for students to be quick to make excuses for their actions or to blame others. I always remind students to *check out the hand*.

When we place blame by pointing a finger at someone, only one finger is pointing in that person's direction; the other three are pointing back at us. This visual of fingers pointing back at themselves gives students an opportunity to consider the role they play in any situation. We can also remind our students that they cannot control someone else's behavior in a situation. What they *can* control is the part they specifically play. We can ask them to consider, "What did *you* do or not do in this situation? What did *you* say, or neglect to say, that could have been more responsible?" The responses to these questions can increase students' awareness that they can make choices to ensure a positive outcome. When they make poor choices, the response to these questions can foster accountability, a crucial aspect of responsible decision making that we can model and teach our students.

An Accountability Process Is Useful

Accountability is a buzz word in education today, but it is an important concept. We have accountability expectations and measures in place from the school board to the district office, to the leadership team at the school site, and the staff in individual classrooms. Educational blogger Justin Tarte (2014) suggests,

> With all of these levels of accountability, we have to ensure we don't lose sight of what our main purpose as educators is; preparing students to be autonomous and independent thinkers. . . . So at the end of the day, let's all assume accountability and let's stop pointing fingers, and let's get to work because I think we all know there's a lot that needs to be done.

I think most of us would agree with Tarte's assessment. Accountability can be associated with different things and different people at different times. Schools nationwide are responsible for producing an accountability report that uses specific data to account for school performance. Administrators and teachers take steps to improve when areas of concern or need for improvement are found. In our classrooms, an accountability process is useful also. Our students can benefit from using such a process, having made a poor choice or irresponsible decision. Figure 7.2 illustrates a three-step process that can serve as a guide in teaching our students to be accountable for their behavior.

FIGURE 7.2

Accountability Process

1. Own It
2. Seek Sincere Forgiveness
3. Make It Right

STEP 1

The first step in an accountability process related to behavior and choices is to own one's irresponsible or poor choice. Our students will benefit from learning to say, "I messed up," "I blew it," or "I was wrong." An ideal way for them to learn this is to allow them to watch us admit we are at fault when we've made an error. I remember observing a class in which the student informed the teacher that her math was incorrect in the example on the board. Even though the teacher argued that it was not, I could see her realize the student was right. She just erased that example and went on to use another one. Unfortunately, this teacher missed a valuable opportunity to model and teach accountability. Furthermore, when we model and teach *owning it,* we also help kids to be specific about the behavior they are owning. For example, if a student uses profanity in class and simply says, "My bad," it isn't as meaningful as, "My bad. I shouldn't have cussed in class." This specificity makes ownership of the behavior more personal and sets up the student for the next step in the process.

STEP 2

Step 2 is to seek sincere forgiveness. *Sincere* is the essential word. Early in my career, I was very proud of myself when I suggested to a student that he own his poor choice after being disrespectful to his PE teacher. After he verbally admitted that he was in fact disrespectful, I proposed that it is was now necessary for him to apologize. He was resistant but agreed. Again, I patted myself on the back and followed him to observe the apology. He approached the PE teacher, saying, "I'm sorry about today." The teacher then asked, "Why are you saying you're sorry?" The student replied, "'Cuz Mrs. T told me to." The PE teacher said, "Come back when you mean it," and all the wind went out of my sails! I had not helped the student internalize and personalize accountability when I asked him to apologize without ensuring that he was sincere in saying he was sorry and asking for forgiveness. His apology also lacked meaning because he didn't specify the behavior related to his poor choice. He said I'm sorry "about today," when "because I talked back to you and then left class" would have been much more appropriate and meaningful.

This specificity can illuminate the difference between an external locus of control and an internal one. If a student's motivation to do the right thing is outside of himself or herself, then the ultimate lesson of accountability is often lost. When students function with an external locus of control, it is common for them to blame others or attribute negative situations to something outside themselves, eliminating the likelihood of an authentic apology. When, instead, we create opportunities for students to work from an internal locus of control, they realize they actually have influence over situations in their lives.

STEP 3

The third step in an effective accountability process is to make it right, meaning two things. First, we need to make sure students understand that even when they take responsibility for a wrongdoing, it may come with consequences or a need for restitution. It is empowering for students to be asked to think through and suggest appropriate consequences or restitution given the situation. Again, it helps them to function from their internal locus of control. Second, if students, or any person for that matter, own their behavior and seek sincere forgiveness, but go right back out and repeat the same behavior, then the owning and apology become meaningless. We can guide our students to develop an action plan that helps them avoid repeating the same offense. Our method may be as simple as providing a reflection page in which the student documents his or her ownership of the behavior, the efforts to make genuine amends, and then a plan to choose differently in the future. Figure 7.3 provides a template that might be useful for better decision making, seeking forgiveness, and making it right.

FIGURE 7.3 Accountability Reflection

I made a poor choice when I _____

_____

In order to seek sincere forgiveness, I will or I have _____

_____

My plan to make it right and choose a more positive behavior next time:

Consequences or restitution: _____

_____

Action plan—be specific about steps you will take to choose differently given a similar situation: _____

_____

_____

CHECK IN CHECK OUT FORMS HELP STUDENTS TO INTRINSICALLY EVALUATE AND MONITOR THEIR BEHAVIOR

Another evidence-based practice that's effective in helping younger students be cognizant of their behavior and decisions is the use of a check in check out (CICO) form. The use of a CICO form can help students be aware of and allow them to reflect on the choices they make that result in positive behavior. Such behaviors might be directly associated with expected behaviors adopted within the school or classroom. The U.S. Department of Education's Office of Special Education Programs promotes Positive Behavioral Interventions and Supports (PBIS). PBIS is an evidence-based practice designed as a multi-tiered system of supports (MTSS) framework that can be implemented schoolwide. Figure 7.4 illustrates an example of a CICO form provided by PBIS (OSEP Technical Assistance Center, 2018). The columns include a rating scale per period (P1, P2, etc.).

FIGURE 7.4

CICO Daily Progress Report						
Name: _____ Date: ___ / ___ / _____		**Rating Scale** 2 = Met all expectations 1 = Met some expectations 0 = Did not meet expectations				
	P1	**P2**	**P3**	**P4**	**P5**	**P6**
Safe	0 1 2	0 1 2	0 1 2	0 1 2	0 1 2	0 1 2
Respectful	0 1 2	0 1 2	0 1 2	0 1 2	0 1 2	0 1 2
Responsible	0 1 2	0 1 2	0 1 2	0 1 2	0 1 2	0 1 2
Total Points						
CICO_SWIS Goal: _____% Points Earned: _____ Points Possible: _____ Goal Met: __YES ___NO Parent/Guardian Signature: _____						

online resources ⬀ Available for download at **resources.corwin.com/StartWithTheHeart**

A more detailed CICO form for students who require a more controlled approach or Tier 2 level of support will provide specific positive behaviors (see Figure 7.5).

Daily Progress Report						
"Social and Academic Instructional Groups" (sample coping skills group)	**Name: _____** **Date: ___ / ___ / _____**					
EXPECTATIONS	**P1**	**P2**	**P3**	**P4**	**P5**	**P6**
Safe *Label feeling* *Use deep breathing*	0 1 2	0 1 2	0 1 2	0 1 2	0 1 2	0 1 2
Respectful *Use calm words with your peers*	0 1 2	0 1 2	0 1 2	0 1 2	0 1 2	0 1 2
Responsible *Let teacher know feeling if above yellow*	0 1 2	0 1 2	0 1 2	0 1 2	0 1 2	0 1 2
Total Points						
Teacher Initials						

CICO forms help students to intrinsically evaluate and monitor their behavior in the classroom. According to Debbie Malone (2015), writing on social and emotional learning,

> [T]he best way to foster this skill is to present students with choices in a variety of contexts. . . . Give students a range of options for completing and submitting assignments. For example, rather than having the whole class write an essay about the book they've just finished reading, give them the opportunity to, alternatively, propose a different way to show or explain what they've learned—such as giving a class presentation, creating a video, or building a website. When teaching a new concept, ask students to think of other methods they can use to complete the same task. Avoid giving directives, and instead, encourage exploration of the rationale and value behind different strategies.

The intent of a CICO form goes beyond completion of the form; it is the relationship between the adult and the student in completing and evaluating the form that creates connection and provides opportunities to reinforce prosocial behaviors. This type of approach is especially effective when norms have been established for a student-centered classroom in which students are assured that their opinions and ideas matter. Such norms may also help students be responsible in regard to their use of electronic devices.

TEACH THEM TO USE TECHNOLOGY RESPONSIBLY

Technology is a powerful educational tool that can and should be used in classrooms across the nation as a modality for gathering data, facilitating research, and engaging in productive discourse. Because many classrooms today are technology rich, we can facilitate opportunities for our students to begin to monitor how and when they use their devices, as well as when to set them aside in order to engage in real-time conversation with another human being. Lessons can be designed based on benefits of artificial intelligence within various content areas, as well as the downside of overusing one's devices at the expense of relationships or personal communication.

With our direction and instruction, opportunities can be created for students to practice regulating the time they spend on electronic devices. Beginning in elementary school, we can assign "technology logs" in which students record their actual usage over a period of a few days. Then, in class, they review their logs and set a goal to decrease time spent on their phone, computer, or gaming device by a specific amount. After another few days, small group discussions can be assigned during which students share their logs with each other, evaluate how close they've come to meeting their goals, and recognize what choices they've made that led to goal achievement. Students who did not meet their goal might brainstorm choices they can make to achieve better results the following week. This technique works well for middle and high school students, as well.

Additionally, a lesson for secondary students might be based on digital citizenship, in which we teach them to use technology responsibly. It is important that young people understand their digital footprint follows them. According to Ana Homayoun, author of *Social Media Wellness: Helping Tweens and Teens Thrive in an Unbalanced Digital World*, "[I]t remains our responsibility to help students understand that their online and real-life experiences and interactions are more intertwined than they've been led to believe" (p. 14). This intertwining of our students' online and real-life experiences and interactions can have unintentional adverse consequences if our students remain unaware of the connection. I have found young people will say and do things through texting or social media that they would not say or do in face-to-face situations. Students might make a sexually provocative request of another person through a text, or send a nude picture of themselves or a friend. I remember a student who came into my office in tears because a classmate had received a nude picture of her. When I asked how she thought this might have happened, she said that she actually sent the picture to her boyfriend a year ago. She said the photo was meant for his eyes only. But she had recently broken up with him and he was angry, so he sent the picture out to everyone on his contact list to embarrass her. It took some time to help this student realize that although her ex-boyfriend made a poor choice and would experience consequences, she had to acknowledge the choice she had made in sending him the picture in the first place, to own that choice, and to accept that the consequences of that choice meant many people eventually saw the photo.

In addition to teaching young people the risks and potential consequences of being irresponsible with what they say or post, we can also teach them the risk of becoming preoccupied with their phones, video or online games, or computers. Students, and adults alike, can become dependent on, or addicted to, their electronic devices. Robert Lustig (2018), a professor at the University of Southern California and author of *The Hacking of the American Mind*, tweeted this about technology: "It's not a drug, but it might as well be. It works the same way.... [I]t has the same results." As a researcher, Lustig studies the addictive effect of sugar and heroin on our brains. In his work, he has found that our brains respond in a similar way to technology. He says, "Technology, like all other 'rewards', can over release dopamine, overexcite and kill neurons, leading to addiction." The good news is that students can learn skills leading to responsible use of electronic devices. Therefore, if we provide knowledge and opportunities for awareness and the practice of digital responsibility, our students are less likely to experience negative outcomes.

ENGAGE STUDENTS IN THE PRACTICE OF AUTONOMY

Finally, our students' opportunities for making choices, applying a decision-making process, and practicing accountability are certainly affected by our instructional styles and approach. For example, as Nicolas Yoder (2014) explains in a brief on the topic of teaching the whole child:

> *Responsibility and choice* refers to the degree to which teachers allow students to make responsible decisions about their work in their classroom. The teacher creates a classroom environment where democratic norms are put into place and where students provide meaningful input into the development of the norms and procedures of the classroom as well as the

academic content or how the academic content is learned. Democratic norms do not mean that everything the students say gets done, but the teacher provides structures so that the students have a voice in the classroom. Teachers give students controlled and meaningful choices. In other words, teachers should not give students a "free for all" but provide specific choices students can select from during lessons and activities, in which students are held accountable for their decisions. (p. 12)

Educators who are student centered, practice supportive control, and create democratic environments are more likely to help students engage in the practice of autonomy (having latitude over one's decisions or freedom from external control) and develop responsible decision-making skills. Conversely, when educators are authoritarian in style, telling students what to do and when to do it, and delivering instruction in a "sit and get" approach, they neglect an opportunity for students to experience active engagement and metacognition, or an awareness and understanding of one's thought processes. All of these skills are essential to students' understanding of and responsibility for their own learning.

When we give students the power of autonomy in school, it can help them transfer responsible decision-making skills to their real-world experiences. Various approaches exist that support autonomy. Stefanou, Perencevich, DiCintio, and Turner (2004) define three distinct features of autonomous support: organizational, procedural, and cognitive. They suggest that effective instruction includes providing student autonomy in all three ways:

> We suggest that, although choice and decision making are fundamental, more than simple choices about tasks or roles are necessary to influence students' decisions to become engaged in academic tasks. Activities that support organizational or procedural autonomy may be necessary but insufficient to promote student engagement. Cognitive autonomy support may be the essential ingredient without which motivation and engagement may not be maximized. (p. 109)

They also provide examples of each style of support, which include choosing evaluation procedures and taking responsibility for due dates, choosing materials for class projects, and finding different solutions to problems.

Reflect on your approach to engage students in activities that increase good decision-making skills. How have you empowered your students to own their choices? How do you provide opportunities for students to experience and exercise autonomy? What does your interaction with students look like? As you answer these questions, please write your thoughts and reflections:

Engaging Students and Increasing Good Decision-Making Skills

_____

_____

_____

_____

_____

_____

_____

_____

_____

_____

_____

_____

_____

_____

online resources ⟍ Available for download at **resources.corwin.com/StartWithTheHeart**

In all phases of their lives, students will benefit from developing skills that lead to responsible decision making. We can empower our students to understand the strength that lies within them to take control of their own lives through responsible choices.

For the last time, in the boxes that follow, you'll hear from students sharing what they think you should know about responsible decision making and their suggestions for teaching the competency.

What You Should Know . . . Responsible Decision Making

Straight From the Hearts of Students

- I like it when teachers give me responsibility in the classroom.

- I make good choices.

- I learn from my mistakes.

- My teachers could support me if they knew what behaviors I participate in.

- I can handle my responsibilities most of the time.

- I think I am responsible. I cannot say for certain though as I am only 13 and am me, so I can't make an unbiased opinion.

- I have okay levels of responsibility. Sometimes I need to know right from wrong.

- If I do something wrong, I know it and am accountable for it. I know a lot of people who don't know what that means.

- I think I'm extremely responsible and get frustrated when people second-guess me.

- I need adults to be kind if I make a bad choice. They can still teach me something without being rude.

- I can easily avoid risky behaviors.

- I want my teachers to know the risky acts that go on.

- It helps me when teachers give me reminders or have a calendar up in the room with assignment due dates.

- I am not responsible whatsoever, but I know I need to become more responsible.

- I wish adults would treat us like we can be responsible.

- Your opinions won't make kids change their lifestyle, but if you have real information, then we might change.

- I'm fine with making decisions, but I appreciate when teachers talk to us about choosing the right thing.

- I need to have more responsibility for turning in my assignments and studying for tests.

- I am very responsible, but sometimes it is hard to keep up in every class every day.

- Don't get mad if I mess up. Help me make better decisions, talk me through them.

- I am pretty good at responsibility but not perfect. It helps when my teachers don't give an overwhelming amount of work.

- I have a high responsibility for choices about school, siblings, and homework. But a low responsibility with a lot of other decisions.

- I can handle myself.

- I just need guidance. Sometimes I have to learn the hard way.

Considering your students and the competency of responsible decision making, please identify a student who might have expressed emotions similar to one of those expressed in the "What You Should Know" box. With the knowledge you have today or the insight from reading these messages, please describe a way you might have changed your interaction with this student or with an entire class in order to help him, her, or them to develop the competency of responsible decision making:

_____

_____

_____

_____

_____

Here are the suggestions from students to help educators teach responsible decision making. As you review the suggestions, highlight two or three that resonate with you.

Suggestions From Students . . . Responsible Decision Making

- Notice how we act in class, like our work habits. That shows responsibility and where we need help.

- We should be able to do activities where we try to solve problems.

- Teach us right from wrong. Don't assume we know.

- Teachers should learn how kids think.

- Get to know your students so you can know if they make bad decisions.

- There should be a full explanation of consequences if someone breaks a rule. Enforcement of consequences should also happen, because a lot of the time it doesn't.

- Give examples of kids who went downhill from making bad decisions.

- For students who are very responsible, recognition or rewards make them stay that way.

- Give students reminders of their choices to be responsible instead of nagging them or telling them what to do.

- Teach students if they have even a thought they shouldn't do something, then don't do it.

(Continued)

(Continued)

- Be fair.
- Teach students how to make decisions.
- Give examples of how people can learn from their mistakes.
- Don't be rude or snobby when students make mistakes. Now, it would be different if the mistake was a constant thing.
- Find a way to show the effects of risky behaviors or choices that aren't responsible.
- Pair good decision makers with bad ones.
- Let students who make good choices tutor students about how they make decisions.
- Teach responsibility, but don't pressure kids.

- Teach students not to make a decision for their own gain. They should be asked to think about other people when they make a decision.
- Make resources available to students that help them make good decisions.
- Have people who have gotten in trouble for breaking the law come in and talk to students.
- Do something with your students that is responsible, like a campus clean-up day or a field trip to a homeless shelter to feed people.
- Teachers give too much time for late work. If you are strict about homework, students would do better getting it in.

Please list below some strategies you might use to foster the highlighted suggestions or to correct current instructional practices that inhibit them. Don't forget to brainstorm potential strategies with a colleague if you have difficulty thinking of strategies on your own.

- *Student suggestion:*

  _____

  _____

  _____

  o *Potential strategy:*

  _____

  _____

  _____

- *Student suggestion:*

  _____

  _____

  _____

○ *Potential strategy:*

_____

_____

_____

• *Student suggestion:*

_____

_____

_____

○ *Potential strategy:*

_____

_____

_____

As we conclude this chapter, please share one behavior, action, or instructional tactic that you will start, one that you will stop, and one that you will continue in regard to decision making:

Start, Stop, Continue . . . Responsible Decision Making

I will START:
I will STOP:
I will CONTINUE:

1. Consider any given school day and approximate the number of choices you make bell to bell. Now, compare that with an estimate of the number of choices students make during the school day. What do you notice?

2. Can you visualize implementing some sort of Healthy Choices group or club at your school? What might it look like?

3. How might explicitly teaching responsible decision making impact academic achievement for all students?

4. In your opinion, what is the correlation between providing opportunities for student choice and responsible decision making? Now, back up your opinion with one piece of evidence.

5. Do you currently teach a decision-making strategy to your students? If so, please describe. If not, which of the suggested strategies mentioned in this chapter appealed to you, and why?

6. Accountability reflections are intended to provide students with an opportunity to reflect on their behavior and make positive change. What is the downside of using accountability reflections punitively, rather than as a positive intervention?

---

online resources ↘ Available for download at **resources.corwin.com/StartWithTheHeart**

CHAPTER 8

Modeling

It Starts With Us

At the beginning of this book, I asked you to join me on a journey to explore the power of connection and the fundamentals of social and emotional learning (SEL) and its impact on academic development. I also suggested that SEL is, more than anything, a way of being. I hope you have been inspired to think of SEL as a philosophy that supports student well-being and learning. We have explored the five SEL competencies—self-awareness, self-management, social awareness, relationship skills, and responsible decision making—and provided ideas and strategies to support your current practice and help your students succeed in academics through applicable relational and life skills. We have explored the use of evidence-based practices that integrate SEL skills into daily school routines. However, embedding SEL in our schools will flourish only if we ensure that educators model each competency and make a concerted effort to care for themselves.

Ensuring that educators are socially and emotionally healthy begins much as it does for our students: with love and respect communicated through connection. Authentic connections must be made starting at the top of the leadership hierarchy. From school boards to the district office, and from administrators to teachers and support staff, we must truly know each other to be able to support each other's personal and professional growth. I recently spoke with Katie, an intelligent and motivated soon-to-be first-year teacher. She completed her student teaching last year, graduated, and was just hired for a third-grade teaching position. I asked her about her student teaching experience, and in reflection she said she learned a lot from her mentor teacher, she loved her students, and was enthusiastic about teaching, but one thing stood out to her as disappointing. Katie told me, "I was a student teacher at the same school for the whole year, and it took almost the entire year for the principal to learn my name. Sometimes I wondered if she even knew who

I was. This made it hard to feel like a true part of the school community." Katie's comment is enlightening. Administrators, consider your staff and how well you know each individual, not only their names, but how they spend time outside of school, their family situations, and challenges or concerns. Staff members, reflect on your relationship with colleagues. How do you connect with them? Do you know why a particular colleague seems angry all of the time, or what the story is behind a colleague's withdrawn demeanor? Seeking to know and understand each other leads to authentic connections that help us feel part of the school community. Katie suggests that new teachers will gain confidence and take pride in their school if they feel they belong. This is true for veteran teachers as well. Feeling part of something positive and profound has ripple effects that impact others positively.

IDENTIFY THE STRENGTHS AND VALUES WITHIN YOUR SCHOOL COMMUNITY

It might be helpful if you and your colleagues identify the strengths and values within your school community, as well as identifying areas that need to be strengthened. Once these are defined, the next step might be to focus on desired outcomes and finding solutions to staff or student morale issues, if they exist. This might be done in small groups at the start of a school year, or at any staff meeting any time during the year. It is important to address concerns before negativity or division permeate the school community. We know it is always about the people. As we seek to develop schools in which all people feel safe, respected, and able to learn and achieve, we need to take time to care about each other and to take care of ourselves so that we do not become overwhelmed, discouraged, or unable to sustain positive relationships.

According to Rollin McCraty of the HeartMath Institute, "Stressed teachers affect their environment, both personal and professional. . . . Often, they are exhausted from lack of sleep and overwork, which has an impact on their preparation, their class demeanor, and their relationships with others in school" (quoted in Israel, 2015, para. 7). The same could be said for stressed administrators, counselors, support staff, parents, and students.

Consider the following reminders as you strengthen your own social and emotional skills to better support these skills in your colleagues and your students:

- *There is only so much within our control.* If we have no control over a specific situation, we must let go and focus our attention on areas in which we can make a positive impact. Sometimes this is difficult to do, but doing so will most likely reduce your stress level. Ask yourself, "What about this situation is within my control?" Based on your answer, ask, "What conditions do I need to have in place in order for the best possible outcome to occur in this situation?" Instead of focusing on what is happening *to* you, ask, "What role do I play in this situation?" Doing this helps us to step out of a victim mentality, which causes stress, and into a survivor mentality, which is empowering and productive.

- *There are only so many hours within a day.* Scheduling responsibilities and activities on a calendar helps us be realistic about what can actually be done in a given day. Initially, schedule *everything,* including meals, exercise, prayer or meditation, and responsibilities to work, family, and community. Often, we have too many things on our calendars. Learning to prioritize what is most important helps relieve stress.

- *Gratitude can change perspective and focus.* Research shows that when we focus on something for which we are grateful, our brains actually release chemicals that make us feel happy (Achor, 2010). You might start each day by journaling or verbally expressing three things (experiences, people, items) for which you are grateful. It helps to write and then post your "gratitudes" in your office or classroom, or even on the bathroom mirror so that you can be reminded on a regular basis.

- *We are all replaceable.* The belief and, therefore, the practice that "I am the only person who can or will . . . [finish the sentence]" places an inordinate amount of stress on a person. Believe it or not, life will go on if something were to happen to us. Work will still be there, and things will still get done. We do not have to carry the entire load or responsibility. Often when we feel this way, it is a result of the choices we make, rather than the responsibility someone else places on us.

- *Breathing is necessary.* Sometimes we get so busy we forget to breathe. Not in the literal sense, but figuratively. If we are moving so fast and doing so much, we will likely feel anxious, stressed out, and out of breath. Remember that taking time to breathe looks different for everyone. For some, it may involve taking an actual breath to re-center and focus oneself. Others need to take time for exercise or to meditate. Some prefer to hike and be in nature to feel at peace, while others find hobbies to be therapeutic. I enjoy reading a good book when I take time to breathe. Whatever it is for you, find it and do it.

- *Stressors (the situations or entities that cause stress) are inevitable; our response makes the difference.* How we respond or react to stressors determines how much stress we actually feel or experience. It is beneficial to body, mind, and spirit to be proactive rather than reactive. Proactive behaviors such as respectful, honest communication and conscious self-discipline can prevent many situations from becoming stressful. People who experience the physical or emotional side effects of stress often react to a situation *after* it happens. We can reduce stress if we are mindful in our thinking in response to an initial situation. Also, if we concentrate on behaving in a way that is calm, kind, and honorable, regardless of the situation, we are more likely to experience less stress. Remember, we cannot control other people or situations, but we do have control over our reactions and responses. When a negative situation is causing stress, it also helps to ask, "What would good look like?" (Creating the Future, 2018). Then, instead of focusing on the problem, the answer to this question helps us focus on the solution. Finally, high school senior Jojo Estrada (2018) suggests that teachers ask themselves, "What if, instead of bottling up our negative experiences, we used them as curriculum to teach our students resiliency and growth?" Appropriately sharing life struggles with our colleagues and even our students may create a more positive outcome from an experience and lessen the stress it causes.

- *Body, mind, and spirit are interconnected and need attention to stay healthy.* We need to remember that our physical, mental, social, and spiritual health all depend on nourishment. If we do not feed ourselves in all areas, we are likely to feel lethargic and edgy and to lack serenity or joy. Review your calendar, and make sure you have scheduled at least a small amount of time for nourishing yourself.

- *There are always resources available.* For school employees who are struggling with mental health issues, family concerns, or personal challenges, schools often have an Employee Assistance Program to offer support. Ask your site administrator or the human resources department at the district level, if you have a need. It is courageous to admit needing help, so don't hesitate. Most of us have experienced times of trial, tribulation, or trauma in different ways and can benefit from accessing school or community resources. One online resource you may find useful is: compassionresiliencetoolkit.org/schools/.

Select one of these reminders and explain how you might apply it to your life:

The point that resonates with me is _____

_____

_____

_____

I can apply this in my life by _____

_____

_____

_____

When we take care of ourselves, we are more likely to be able to model the social and emotional learning competencies we want our students to possess. Modeling is a powerful teaching tool.

OUR STUDENTS WATCH US, CONSTANTLY!

My father-in-law, Phil Trujillo, dedicated his life to education. He served as a teacher, coach, principal, superintendent, and school board member. Sadly, Phil passed away several years ago. His death was an overwhelming loss to our family, as well as to the community. During his funeral, I was not surprised when the church filled with his former students and colleagues. Furthermore, cards poured in from people whose lives had been impacted by "Mr. Trujillo" or "Coach." I was so inspired by the sincere and thoughtful words written on each card. Virtually every person, from former elementary and secondary students and athletes to teachers and coaches who worked with Phil or for him, expressed that although Phil made an impression on their lives as an educator, he made an even bigger impact as a "decent and caring human being." Collectively, they spoke of having a deep respect for him. They said he was influential, a good and fine man.

I remember visiting one of Phil's schools with him when he was superintendent. As he walked down the halls, he greeted students and staff by name. He was polite, kind, and curious about what they were learning or teaching in their classrooms, as well as how things were going at home. I was certain, as I watched his interactions, that every person he greeted felt important and appreciated. He routinely behaved with courtesy and respect, which inspired those within his schools to act in a similar manner. It was the way in which Phil lived his life, his daily actions at school and on the football field or basketball court, that made such a positive impact on his students and colleagues.

Ralph Waldo Emerson is credited with having said, "What you do speaks so loud that I cannot hear what you say." Our students watch us, constantly! They watch us in the classroom and the hallways. They watch us interact with our colleagues and with other students. We can teach them valuable lessons in the way in which we live our lives on a daily basis. The accompanying table suggests ways to model life skills and interpersonal behavior.

EDUCATOR BEHAVIORS	
Self-Awareness	• Identifying and expressing emotions appropriately and respectfully, but not being afraid to admit our feelings.
	• Sharing talents or strengths with our students and colleagues.
	• Providing opportunities for students to observe us demonstrating our strengths and talents with confidence, and an appropriate dose of humility.
	• Acknowledging when we are unsure of something or confused about a situation.
	• Taking time to determine why we do what we do.

(Continued)

- Acknowledging that we don't know what we don't know, but that we are willing to learn.
- Noticing the positive or negative effect our emotions have on others. Nourishing the positive and finding ways to avoid the negative.
- Asking for help or support when we are overwhelmed, anxious, or unsure of a situation.
- Being aware of our values and actively putting them into practice.

Self-Management	<ul><li>Controlling our emotions even when we are anxious, frustrated, overwhelmed, or angry.</li><li>Communicating with respect and kindness regardless of the situation and who it involves, be it students or colleagues.</li><li>Choosing to say no or set boundaries if additional work responsibilities become overwhelming.</li><li>Refraining from gossiping or sharing personal information about other staff members.</li><li>Talking respectfully about colleagues at all times, even when we don't think students are present.</li><li>Taking a deep breath before we respond to another, to demonstrate thoughtfulness, or self-control if we are frustrated.</li><li>Stopping ourselves when we begin to gossip or talk about a colleague.</li><li>Redirecting a conversation that is negative or demeaning to students or colleagues.</li></ul>
Social Awareness	<ul><li>Practicing equity by learning about those who are different from ourselves, whether in ethnicity, ability, gender identity, socioeconomic status, sexuality, family customs, or traditions.</li><li>Accepting others with a show of support, encouragement, and kindness.</li><li>Standing up to harassment, bullying, or teasing and taunting by setting expectations for kindness and respect schoolwide and following through with restorative practices that foster acceptance, compassion, and accountability.</li><li>Creating opportunities for cultural awareness schoolwide so that students can learn and respect the backgrounds of others, by sharing and celebrating our own customs and traditions and giving our students an opportunity to do so as well.</li><li>Seeking to understand the perspectives of others by asking nonjudgmental questions and exposing ourselves to situations out of our comfort zone.</li><li>Participating in home visits to learn more about the situations in which our students live.</li><li>Responding from a place of love, as opposed to judgment or fear when we don't understand a person's actions or behaviors.</li></ul>

Relationship Skills	• Acknowledging students and colleagues daily with the use of their name and a sincere greeting.
	• Connecting kinesthetically by routinely shaking hands, fist bumping, or slapping high fives—with both our students and colleagues.
	• Building trust by practicing respectful communication, seeking to understand, and accepting others.
	• Giving colleagues and students a genuine second chance when they express such a need.
	• Writing notes of appreciation to colleagues, students, and parents.
	• Respecting authority and striving to see our supervisors' perspective.
	• Taking or making time to listen when a colleague or student has a concern.
	• Laughing with colleagues and students.
	• Sharing kind thoughts, encouragement, and even food at times.
Responsible Decision Making	• Acting in a respectful manner, even when we don't feel respected.
	• Using a decision-making process in a public manner so that others might observe the process in action.
	• Creating random acts of kindness.
	• Refraining from engaging in gossip, rumors, and discussions that are negative.
	• Being aware of our actions outside of school and ensuring that they are responsible and appropriate, including postings and pictures on social media sites.
	• Taking care of our mental and physical health. Joining colleagues or students for mindfulness activities or physical exercise.
	• Eating nutritiously.
	• Driving safely in the school parking lot.
	• Refraining from using profanity.
	• Spending quality time with our families and knowing that five years from now they will still be the center of our world.

 Available for download at **resources.corwin.com/StartWithTheHeart**

We all benefit from treating others with kindness, helping one another, and acting responsibly. Modeling these behaviors demonstrates and reiterates to our students that these competencies are more than a new initiative or skills to be used only in school. When we strive to be self-aware and responsible and to practice self-control, when we value building and maintaining relationships with others, when we accept others without intentional bias or judgment, and when we take care of our own social and emotional well-being, our students will be more inclined to listen, learn, and emulate these actions. Once we make a sincere effort to practice behaviors that make up the competencies, we will be better prepared to teach social and emotional learning skills.

DEVELOP THE WHOLE CHILD BY INVESTING IN A MULTI-TIERED SYSTEM OF SUPPORTS

When schools adopt social and emotional learning as a philosophy, it makes sense that they continue to develop the whole child by investing in a multi-tiered system of supports (MTSS). Within this framework, evidence-based practices can be implemented and sustained to support positive student behaviors and provide systematic interventions as necessary. As educators, we are constantly being asked to adopt new initiatives; sometimes they last, and sometimes they don't. Implementing SEL and making connections with our students and colleagues to promote interpersonal relationships, life skills, and academic achievement is an initiative that serves humankind. Integrating MTSS provides sustainability for this initiative. Ashley Greenwald, project director for Nevada's PBIS Technical Assistance Center, explains it well:

> Teachers, school teams, districts, and state departments often bring on new initiatives to address recurrent issues, be that behavioral or academic. The challenge with implementing new initiatives each year is that the interventions are never implemented to fidelity, thereby never achieving the intended student outcomes. Rather than rolling out plans because they are popular, implementing a framework using multi-tiered systems of support significantly increases the likelihood of favorable student outcomes, no matter the initiative. MTSS evaluates existing data, assesses the effectiveness of current practices, uses data to make decisions, selects evidence-based practices, and monitors outcomes throughout the school year to determine effectiveness. By investing time and energy into MTSS systems and data components, the practices become effective and efficient, the money spent on new initiatives and trainings decreases, and student outcomes are achieved. MTSS can take any evidence-based practice across any domain and support its implementation to fidelity. (personal interview, August 1, 2018)

Schools have a choice of many evidence-based practices to adopt as positive behavior intervention programs, SEL curricula, or trauma-informed practice based on students' and schools' needs. Kristen Amundson, the president and chief executive officer of the National Association of State Boards of Education, said, "A program that works swimmingly in State A might be a colossal failure in State B . . . . You have to respect local differences and listen. You have to involve parents, and you have to listen to teachers. The goal is to have something take root. But before that can happen, everybody has to agree that this approach matters for our kids" (quoted in Aspen Institute, 2017, p. 12).

WEBSITES FOR EFFECTIVE AND PROMISING PROGRAMS AND EVIDENCE-BASED PRACTICES

We, as administrators, teachers, and support staff, are part of the *everybody* to which Amundson refers. In addition to listening to everybody, we also must pay attention to our data. Every school possesses specific information that tells us the type of promising practice or evidence-based program that best aligns with our targeted needs, demographics, and desired outcome. There is no sense in adopting a program without taking these data into account. Likewise, we must move forward incrementally as we adopt practices and programs, in order for sustainable positive change to take place. It is natural for people, both adults and students, to push back if they are confronted with too much change too quickly. Steps taken in increments, however, are more likely to create open minds and open hearts. Finally, any program or practice adopted is only as good as the fidelity with which it is implemented. Fidelity requires investment and consistency of all stakeholders (even if only in increments), and it also requires intermittent progress monitoring and commitment to make modifications or adjustments as needed. Take time now to peruse at least two of the following websites for effective and promising practices and evidence-based programs, keeping the aforementioned information in mind:

- https://casel.org/guide/
- https://www.evidenceforessa.org/
- https://www.cdc.gov/healthyschools/wscc/index.htm
- http://www.promisingpractices.net
- https://ies.ed.gov/ncee/wwc/
- https://www.samhsa.gov/capt/tools-learning-resources/finding-evidence-based-programs
- https://www.air.org/resource/crosswalk-aligning-evidence-based-clearinghouses-essa-tiers-evidence
- https://www.cdc.gov/violenceprevention/youthviolence/prevention.html

Reflect below on specific programs that stood out to you as potentially applicable for your school. Suppose a discussion is taking place at your school in which all staff members are asked to take part in an effort to adopt a SEL program using evidence-based practices. Please write here about two of the programs you considered, why each might be appropriate for your school, and how each might meet the needs of your students:

1. *Program:*

   _____

   _____

   _____

   _____

   a. *Why:*

   _____

   _____

   _____

   _____

   b. *How:*

   _____

   _____

   _____

   _____

2. *Program:*

   _____

   _____

   _____

   _____

   a. *Why:*

   _____

   _____

   _____

   _____

   b. *How:*

   _____

   _____

   _____

   _____

Numerous resources are available to you and your school to support students, as evidenced in the previously mentioned websites. Sadly, many of these programs are needed because so many of our students experience mental health challenges, struggle with learning, and lack hope. According to the 2017 Youth Risk Behavior Survey, 33.5% of surveyed students reported experiencing persistent feelings of sadness or hopelessness (Centers for Disease Control and Prevention, 2018). Suicide rates for young people are skyrocketing. According to an article in *USA Today*, "The suicide rate for white children and teens between 10 and 17 was up 70% between 2006 and 2016, the latest data analysis available from the Centers for Disease Control and Prevention. Although black children and teens kill themselves less often than white youth do, the rate of increase was higher—77%" (Saker, 2018). In May 2018, CNN reported that in the first 21 weeks of 2018, there were 23 school shootings in which someone was hurt or killed (Walker, 2018). These statistics are daunting, and they remind us that the work we do is vitally important. We do not see statistics; we see human beings. We do not see hopelessness; we see hope, because we can *be* hope.

Tony Dungy (2007) says it best: "It's about the journey—mine and yours—and the lives we can touch, the legacy we can leave and the world we can change for the better" (p. xv). By embracing all you've discovered on this journey, by living in a way that values humankind, and by integrating strategies to practice social and emotional learning as life skills for your students and yourself, you can and will make the world better. As you prepare to close this book, I hope you felt encouraged and inspired as you explored each chapter. I hope you reflected on the people in your lives and the positive difference you can make in the lives of your students and colleagues. I hope you realize that we *are* hope, because we *are* educators. Finally, remember:

We can truly make a difference

Starting with the Heart, our fervent vow

And with SEL as the foundation

We can ignite HOPE in our schools now!

1. Inside the circle below, please list situations, behaviors, or actions within the school day that are completely within your control. Then, outside the circle list things that are out of your control. Reflect on your results and reflect on the items on which you spend most of your energy. Contrast that with where you should or would like to spend your energy.

2. For what or whom are you grateful, and why?

3. Which "reminder" to strengthen your own social and emotional learning resonates most with you, and why?

4. How can modeling breathing, meditation, or gratitude have a positive effect on your classroom environment and student achievement?

5. In the "Educator Behavior" table in this chapter, highlight or underline one behavior from each competency that you will practice mindfully. Explain at least one of your choices.

6. Explain at least one way in which you make a positive difference within your school community.

7. Consider the SEAD MTSS Integrated Model on the opposite page. Reflect and discuss ways in which this model may be used or modified to facilitate integration of social, emotional, and academic development within your school district or site.

Social, Emotional, and Academic Development (SEAD) Through the
Lens of a Multi-Tiered System of Supports (MTSS)

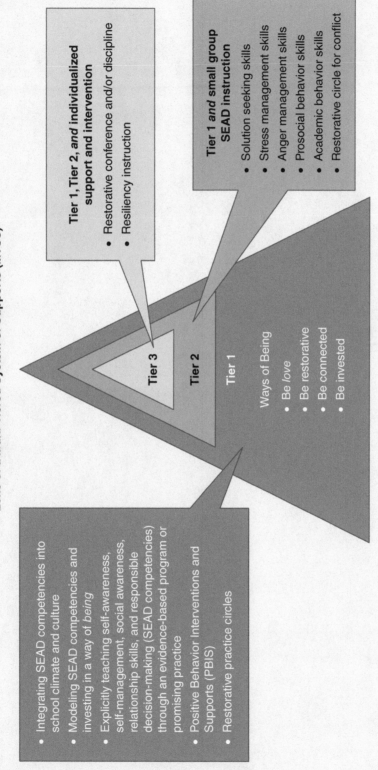

Tier 1, Tier 2, *and* individualized support and intervention
- Restorative conference and/or discipline
- Resiliency instruction

Tier 1 *and* small group SEAD instruction
- Solution seeking skills
- Stress management skills
- Anger management skills
- Prosocial behavior skills
- Academic behavior skills
- Restorative circle for conflict

Tier 3

Tier 2

Tier 1

Ways of Being
- Be *love*
- Be *restorative*
- Be *connected*
- Be *invested*

- Integrating SEAD competencies into school climate and culture
- Modeling SEAD competencies and investing in a way of *being*
- Explicitly teaching self-awareness, self-management, social awareness, relationship skills, and responsible decision-making (SEAD competencies) through an evidence-based program or promising practice
- Positive Behavior Interventions and Supports (PBIS)
- Restorative practice circles

online resources ⌐Ⅎ Available for download at **resources.corwin.com/StartWithTheHeart**

Acknowledgments

First, to you, the reader: Thank you for investing in this journey with me. It was important to me to write a book that would speak to your heart, while providing you with valuable information and practical strategies. If I accomplished this goal, it was due only to the support and contribution of the following people:

- Sharalee Jorgensen, godmother, aunt, and editor extraordinaire! This book took shape, only because of you.

- Judy Williams, my mom, my friend. You made yourself available to read and reread at any given moment. Thanks, to you and Dad, and Jaime, too, for *always* being there!

- Rene Townsend, author, former principal, and superintendent. Your "in the trenches" insight was invaluable!

- Jessica Allan, Lucas Schleicher, Mia Rodriguez, and Tori Mirsadjadi. In my eyes, you are Corwin's finest editing team. Thank you for your belief in this book from the start! And Amy Marks, you are something special. Thank you!

- Telsche, Ashlee, Alecia, Eric, Krystal, Nick, McKayla, Charlie, Cisco, Kat, Sarah, Katie, Callie, and Bryan's mom, Shirley. Your willingness to contribute to and support this project touched my heart and made this book come alive. Thank you.

- David Trujillo, my husband and best friend, and our children, Corey and Dani. You are the joy of my heart! Thank you all for your belief in me and your constant support, insight, and encouragement. I love you.

Many of the anecdotes that I shared throughout the book were based on students who have touched my heart and made me a better teacher and leader. Names that I acknowledged here are real, but there are others for whom I changed names or left unnamed to protect their privacy. Finally, as you could tell from reading this book, I believe in love. All glory goes to the original source of Love: to my God, Thank You.

Publisher's Acknowledgments

Melissa A. Campbell
4th Grade Mathematics Teacher
Williams Avenue Elementary School
Fort Payne, Alabama

Dr. Ursula Harris
Educator
Jackson Public Schools
Jackson, Mississippi

Linda Keteyian
Teacher
Detroit Public Schools
Detroit, Michigan

Saundra Mouton
International Baccalaureate Coordinator
Briarmeadow Charter School
Houston, Texas

Dr. Tanna H. Nicely
Executive Principal
South Knoxville Elementary
Knoxville, Tennessee

Ellen S. Perconti
Superintendent
Mary M. Knight and Grapeview School Districts
Elma, Washington

Cathy Sosnowski
Teacher
Central Connecticut State University
New Britain, Connecticut

References

Abdul-Jabbar, K. (2017). *Coach Wooden and Me: Our 50-Year Friendship On and Off the Court*. New York, NY: Hachette.

Achor, S. (2010). *The Happiness Advantage: The Seven Principles of Positive Psychology That Fuel Success and Performance at Work*. New York, NY: Crown.

Adams, S. (2014, November 12). The 10 skills employers most want in 2015 graduates. *Forbes*. Retrieved from https://www.forbes.com/sites/susanadams/2014/11/12/the-10-skills-employers-most-want-in-2015-graduates/#3e86d21c2511

Alexander, M. (2012). *The New Jim Crow*. New York, NY: New Press.

Amiel, H. F. (2016, January 1). Henri Frederic Amiel quotes. *Brainy Quote*. Retrieved from https://www.brainyquote.com/quotes/henri_frederic_amiel_148230

Angelou, M. (2014). *Rainbow in the Cloud: The Wisdom and Spirit of Maya Angelou*. New York, NY: Random House.

Aspen Institute. (2017). *How Learning Happens: Supporting Students' Social Emotional and Academic Development*. Retrieved from https:\\assets.aspeninstitute.org: https://assets.aspeninstitute.org/content/uploads/2018/01/FINAL_2017_Aspen_InterimReport_Update.pdf

Aspen Institute. (2018, May 1). *Pursuing Social and Emotional Development Through a Racial Equity Lens: A Call to Action*. Retrieved from https://assets.aspeninstitute.org/content/uploads/2018/05/Aspen-Institute_Framing-Doc_Call-to-Action.pdf

Aspen Institute National Commission on Social, Emotional and Academic Development. (2017a, February). NCSEAD. Retrieved from https://assets.aspeninstitute.org/content/uploads/2017/02/NCSEAD-Value-Statements.pdf

Aspen Institute National Commission on Social, Emotional, and Academic Development. (2017b, May 18). Facebook "LIVE" interview with Eric Gordon & Antwan Wilson. Retrieved from https://www.aspeninstitute.org/videos/ncseads-facebook-live-interview-eric-gordon/

Bandura, A. (1998). Self-Efficacy. *Encyclopedia for Mental Health*. Academic Press. p. 71

Barker, E. (2014, June 30). How to motivate yourself: 3 Steps backed by science. *Time*. Retrieved from http://time.com/2933971/how-to-motivate-yourself-3-steps-backed-by-science/

Belfield, C., Bowden, A. B., Klapp, A., Levin, H., Shand, R., & Zander, S. (2015). The economic value of social and emotional learning. *Journal of Benefit-Cost Analysis*, *6*(3), 508–544.

Bradberry, T., & Greaves, J. (2009). *Emotional Intelligence 2.0*. San Diego, CA: Talent Smart.

Brown, D., & Skinner, D. (2007, November 3). Brown-Skinner model for building trust with at-risk students. *National Forum of Applied Educational Research Journal, 20*(3). Retrieved from http://www.nationalforum.com/Electronic%20Journal%20Volumes/Brown,%20Donald%20Donald%20Brown-Skinner%20Model%20for%20Building%20trust%20with%20At-Risk%20Students.pdf

Centers for Disease Control and Prevention. (2016, April 1). About adverse childhood experiences. Retrieved from https://www.cdc.gov/violenceprevention/acestudy/about_ace.html

Centers for Disease Control and Prevention. (2018, June 14). CDC releases Youth Risk Behavior Survey results and trends report. Retrieved from https://www.cdc.gov/healthyyouth/data/yrbs/pdf/trendsreport.pdf

Character Counts! (2017, July 12). Greatest quotes on character, reputation and character education. Retrieved from https://charactercounts.org/greatest-quotes-on-character-reputation-and-character-education/

Collaborative for Academic, Social, and Emotional Learning. (2018, June 30). Core SEL competencies. Retrieved from https://casel.org/core-competencies/

Comer, J. (2005, September 1). Interview. *Making Schools Work With Hedrick Smith*. Retrieved from http://www.pbs.org/makingschoolswork/sbs/csp/jamescomer.html

Creating the Future. (2018, July 16). Core philosophy & values. Retrieved from https://creatingthefuture.org/core-philosophy-values/

The Dalai Lama. (2013). *The Dalai Lama's Little Book of Wisdom*. New York, NY: Harper Collins.

Davis, D. E., Worthington, E. L., Jr., Hook, J. N., Emmons, R. A., Hill, P. C., Bollinger, R. A., & Van Tongeren, D. R. (2013). Humility and the development and repair of social bonds: Two longitudinal studies. *Self and Identity, 12*(1), 58-77.

Duckworth, A. (2016). *Grit: The Power of Passion and Perseverance*. New York, NY: Scribner.

Dungy, T. (2007). *Quiet Strength: The Principles, Practices, and Priorities of a Winning Life*. Carol Stream, IL: Tyndale House.

Durlak, J. A., Weissberg, R. P., Dymnicki, A. B., Taylor, R. D., & Schellinger, K. B. (2011). The impact of enhancing students' social and emotional learning: A meta-analysis of school-based interventions. *Child Development 82*(1): 405–432.

Estrada, J. (2018, July 18). TEDxYouth@MVHS. Retrieved from https://www.youtube.com/watch?v=n2_hIg--h4U

Fields, D. F., & Fields, M. V. (2010, July 20). Learning perspective taking. Retrieved from https://www.education.com/download-pdf/reference/25969/

Greenberg, J. P. (2012, March). Serving Hispanic school-aged children in after school programming: Implications for school social work. *School Social Work Journal, 36*(2), 73–88.

Gregory, A., & Fergus, E.. (2017). Social and emotional learning and equity in school discipline. *The Future of Children, 27*(1), 117–136.

Hattie, J., & Zierer, K. (2018). *10 Mindframes for Visible Learning: Teaching for Success*. New York, NY: Routledge.

Homayoun, A. (2018). *Social Media Wellness: Helping Tweens and Teens Thrive in an Unbalanced Digital World*. Thousand Oaks, CA: Corwin.

Hook, J. N., Davis, D. E., Owen, J., Worthington, E. L., & Utsey, S. O. (2013). Cultural humility: Measuring openness to diverse clients. *Journal of Counseling Psychology, 60*(3), 353–366.

Humility. (2018a, July 20). Retrieved from Merriam-Webster Dictionary: https://www .merriam-webster.com/dictionary/humility

Israel, M. (2015, January 1). From chaos to coherence: Managing stress while teaching. *Education World*. Retrieved from https://www.educationworld.com/a_admin/admin/ admin413.shtml

Jensen, E. (2005). *Teaching With the Brain in Mind*. Alexandria, VA: ASCD.

Jensen, E. (2009). *Teaching With Poverty in Mind: What Being Poor Does to Kids' Brains and What Schools Can Do About It*. Alexandria, VA: ASCD.

Landmark School Outreach. (2018, June 29). Professional development for educators. Retrieved from https://www.landmarkoutreach.org/strategies/sel-self-awareness/

Lustig, R. (2018, February 9). Tweet. Retrieved from https://twitter.com/RobertLustigMD/ status/962032237528018949

Malone, D. (2015, July 8). Responsible decision making: Applying social and emotional learning (SEL) in your classroom. Retrieved from https://blog.edgenuity.com/respon sible-decision-making-applying-social-and-emotional-learning-in-your-classroom/

Marzano, R. J., McNulty, B., & Waters, T. (2005). *School leadership that works*. Alexandria, VA: ASCD.

McBride, B. (2017, August 2). HRC launches major survey for LGBTQ teens. Retrieved from https://www.hrc.org/blog/hrc-launches-major-survey-for-lgbtq-teens

Middleton, Y. (2016, February 28). 100 Unforgettable John Wooden Quotes. Retrieved from addictied2success.com: https://addicted2success.com/quotes/100-unforgettable-john-wooden-quotes/

Mistake. (2018b, August 5). Retrieved from Merriam-Webster Dictionary: https://www .merriam-webster.com/dictionary/mistake

OSEP Technical Assistance Center. (2018, August 1). Positive Behavior Interventions and Supports. Retrieved from nevadapbis.org: nevadapbis.org/isf-resources/

The PE Geek Apps. (2018). *Move It*. Retrieved from https://thepegeek.com/apps/

Pianta, B. H. (2001, March–April). Early teacher-child relationships and the trajectory of children's school outcomes through eighth grade. *Child Development*, *72*, 625–638.

Rajagopal, K. (2011). *Create Success!* Alexandria, VA: ASCD. [Kindle edition]

Rimm-Kaufman, S., & Sandolis, P. A. (2018, July 23). Improving students' relation- ships with teachers to provide essential supports for learning. *American Psychological Association*. Retrieved from https://www.apa.org/education/k12/relationships.aspx

Saker, J. O. (2018, March 19). Teen suicide is soaring. Do spotty mental health and addic- tion treatment share blame? *USA Today*. Retrieved from https://www.usatoday.com/ story/news/politics/2018/03/19/teen-suicide-soaring-do-spotty-mental-health-and- addiction-treatment-share-blame/428148002/

Skiba, R. J., Horner, R. H., Chung, C.-G., Rausch, M. K., May, S. L., & Tobin, R. (2011). Race is not neutral: A national investigation of African American and Latino dispro- portionality in school discipline. *School Psychology Review*, *40*(1), 85–107.

Smith, D., Fisher, D., & Frey, N. (2017). *Better Than Carrots and Sticks: Restorative Practices for Positive Classroom Management*. Alexandria, VA: ASCD. [Kindle edition]

Soul Pancake. (2013, December 19). How to Change the World; Kid President. *(Soul Pancake)* Retrieved from https://www.youtube.com/watch?v=4z7gDsSKUmU

Starr, J. P. (2016, November 30). Taking SEAD to scale: The educator perspective. *The Aspen Institute*. Retrieved from https://www.aspeninstitute.org/blog-posts/ taking-sead-scale-educator-perspective/

Stefanou, C. R., Perencevich, K. C., DiCintio, M., & Turner, J. C. (2004). Supporting autonomy in the classroom: Ways teachers encourage student decision making and ownership. *Educational Psychologist, 39*(2), 97–110.

Tarte, J. (2014, June 8). Life of an educator. Retrieved http://www.justintarte.com/2014/06/accountability-to-whom-finger-pointing.html

Tracy, B. (2011). *No Excuses! The Power of Self Discipline*. New York, NY: Vanguard Press.

Varlas, L. (2018, June). Emotions are the rudder that steers thinking. *Education Update, 60*(6).

Vujicic, N. (2018, June 29). Nick: Bio. Retrieved from https://www.lifewithoutlimbs.org/about-nick/bio/

Walker, S. A. (2018, May 25). 2018 School shootings: A list of incidents that resulted in casualties. *CNN*. Retrieved from https://www.cnn.com/2018/03/02/us/school-shootings-2018-list-trnd/index.html

Wooden, J., & Jamison, S. (1997). *Wooden: A Lifetime of Observations and Reflections On and Off the Court*, 6th ed. New York: Contemporary Books.

Yoder, N. (2014, January 1). *Teaching the Whole Child Instructional Practices That Support Social-Emotional Learning in Three Teacher Evaluation Frameworks*. Center on Great Teachers and Leaders at American Institutes for Research. https://gtlcenter.org/sites/default/files/TeachingtheWholeChild.pdf

Index

Note: Page numbers in *italic* refer to figures.

A SAGE Publishing Company

Helping educators make the greatest impact

CORWIN HAS ONE MISSION: to enhance education through intentional professional learning.

We build long-term relationships with our authors, educators, clients, and associations who partner with us to develop and continuously improve the best evidence-based practices that establish and support lifelong learning.

Solutions *YOU WANT* | Experts *YOU TRUST* | Results *YOU NEED*

EVENTS

>>> INSTITUTES

Corwin Institutes provide large regional events where educators collaborate with peers and learn from industry experts. Prepare to be recharged and motivated!

corwin.com/institutes

ON-SITE PD

>>> ON-SITE PROFESSIONAL LEARNING

Corwin on-site PD is delivered through high-energy keynotes, practical workshops, and custom coaching services designed to support knowledge development and implementation.

corwin.com/pd

>>> PROFESSIONAL DEVELOPMENT RESOURCE CENTER

The PD Resource Center provides school and district PD facilitators with the tools and resources needed to deliver effective PD.

corwin.com/pdrc

ONLINE

>>> ADVANCE

Designed for K–12 teachers, Advance offers a range of online learning options that can qualify for graduate-level credit and apply toward license renewal.

corwin.com/advance

Contact a PD Advisor at (800) 831-6640 or visit www.corwin.com for more information